Set Free

SET FREE

The testimony of Anthony

By: Anthony Krehn

Cover artwork by Eddie "Lowrider"

Disclaimer:
Names and dates have been changed to protect the privacy
of individuals and facilities.

TABLE OF CONTENTS

FORWARD

Set Free is a true story about one who was broken and ravaged by sin. Anthony's childhood was stained by heinous offenses, the kind no child should ever encounter. When Anthony turns away from God and hardens his heart, his life plummets. Sin and rebelliousness take over.

As Anthony's life spirals downward, he indulges in dangerous ventures. His crime leads him to a life sentence. Behind bars, he dives into the only book available to him, the Bible. Anthony encounters the true and living God through the word. When he begins to grasp the love of God, he is overwhelmed and surrenders his life to His Lordship. Anthony shares, "I fell to my knees and asked Jesus to give me a new heart and life. Literally, like honey, the love and peace of God touched my head and ran all the way through my entire body and right into my feet. I broke!"

Anthony relates the time a Pastor comes to the prison to baptize him, "The pastor looked directly at me and laying his hand upon my shoulder said, "We are sending you as a missionary of our church into the darkest places of the world where we ourselves cannot go." As foretold, Anthony is sent to some of the darkest prisons of the world. He does not go alone. He goes with the gospel of peace to share God's message of salvation through faith.

As you read Anthony's testimony you will be riveted by God's mighty power being poured into Anthony's life.

The enemy comes against Anthony and assaults him with physical manifestations. Anthony puts on the armor of God. God wins! Walk with Anthony as he ministers to hardened criminals. Rejoice as you read true stories of surrendered lives that are changed forever. Witness Anthony's struggles and weariness and then be amazed at how his Father God teaches him right in the midst of his pain.

Anthony gives God glory and recognizes his favor, it follows him throughout his days. May your hearts be touched as you are witness to God's tender shepherding of his son. May God be glorified and may your eyes and hearts be opened to a sector of God's people who live behind bars. God is at work!

Susan Jill Ream

INTRODUCTION

Once I was at the facility which was close to my family, a couple of brothers and a sister from my church wanted to come and visit me. All were a blessing, but there was one brother who I recognized immediately...we were both of the same cloth.

After several visits, he began asking me to write out my testimony. I wasn't too thrilled with that idea but each time he came, once a month, he would say the same thing. I continued to shrug off his suggestion.

During one of our visits we were talking about what God was doing in our lives and the Spirit led us to the scripture verse, "The testimony of Jesus is the spirit of prophecy." (Revelation 19:10).

As we were ministering to each other, the Holy Spirit began to reveal to me that our testimony is not who we were while living under sin. Rather, our testimony is who we presently are in Christ. Our testimony is what God has prophesied over us, even from the foundations of the earth, of who we are in Him, and what we can do through Him. Once I saw that, all reservations of writing my testimony were gone. I had no desire to reminisce in my past. *My testimony revolves around what God has done in my life since willingly accepting Him.*

The evening after that visit, I called my mom and she

told me that a woman stopped her at church and asked about me. The woman said that God had placed me upon her heart, and that I needed to write out my testimony. *I have never told my mom that I was even considering writing my testimony! Without a doubt, I knew this was God at work and it was time for people to hear of what God was doing, where most wouldn't think of looking, even behind jail cell walls and barbed wire fences.*

My testimony is not about who I was; rather, it revolves around the Lordship of our resurrected Savior, Jesus Christ. As promised, His power and victory has been seen, handled and witnessed within my life over every trial, tribulation and difficulty that, as believers, we all face. It further revolves around the revelations which enabled me to overcome and place my feet on the neck of every insecurity, fear, wound, hurt and abandonment issues that Satan had given me while I lived under his authority in the free world. "For the thief (Satan) comes only to steal and to kill and destroy; I (Jesus) came that they might have life, and have it more abundantly." (John 10:10)

The accounts you are about to read may not necessarily be in the exact order of events but they are all true.

"For the testimony of Jesus is the spirit of prophecy." (Revelation 19:10) I would like to share with you my testimony of what Jesus has done for me, through me, being more powerful than anything that the devil tried to masquerade by destruction, pain, loneliness and anger in which I lived.

There is a prophecy that I wrote out in Chapter 3 that really impacted my life. I am not sure who the man was that received it from God; I only know that his name was Bill. I just wanted whoever reads this to know, that God did not personally give me this prophecy. I only used it, because it has become so meaningful in my walk.

As you read this, my hope is that if any of it relates to you, you will know that God is not a respecter of persons. As He delivered me, so He will deliver you. The purpose of life is that God's Holy Spirit may reflect Jesus. I pray this will bless you.

Smith Wigglesworth said a very powerful thing, "We are living epistles of Christ, read and know of all men. Our very presence must bring such a witness of the Spirit, that whomever we come into contact with, may know that we are a sent one, a light in the world, a manifestation of the Christ, and last of all a biblical Christian."

I try to live my life by this. God never promises any of us that walking with Him will be easy. In fact, He promises the opposite, but He does promise that He will be with us and that if we walk by the Spirit, in faith, we will get the victory over every circumstance and situation. *I believe this. If I can live in this, then so can you.*

1

A LIFE TAKEN AND A LIFE GIVEN

It all began one night in September when a new acquaintance and I robbed a gas station. He knew the people who owned and ran the establishment, so we decided that he would go in first and shoot the clerk, at which time, I would come in and we would rob the place. He shot and killed the clerk and as we started to take the money, the clerk's brother pulled up and we ran out.

The next morning, a friend woke me up telling me that my description was all over the news. I did not tell him that I took part in the crime; instead, I did what I always did…I lied. My friend convinced me to turn myself in and clear my name. I was fully convinced within myself that I would be able to lie my way out of it.

I called my mom, who was a police dispatcher at the time, and told her that I wanted to turn myself in, but only to the custody of my uncle, who happened to be a police officer.

At the police station, the first thing my uncle did was show me a picture of some guy who I didn't know. I said, "I don't know him." I should have caught on right then, but it was as though something was covering my eyes and I could not perceive what was happening. My uncle then brought me to a room where a detective was sitting. Upon entering the room, it was as if something very powerful came over me. Regardless of what questions they asked, I found myself telling the truth. I couldn't stop it! After being processed and brought to the county jail, I came to my senses and realized that I had just told the cops everything!

After seeing the judge on the TV screen and finding out that I was looking at natural life without the possibility of parole, something inside me broke. Within an hour, I was called out for a clergy visit. I was put in a room divided by super thick glass with a small opening at the bottom through which to speak.

A little, old man walked in to the adjacent room, told me his name, then asked, "Can I pray for you?" *I lost it!* I started to cry and yell at him. I told him that I was looking at natural life and that his prayers were not going to help me at all!

Calmly, he started to pray and no matter how much I wanted to shut him out I was stuck in the room having to listen to the old man ask 'some god' to touch my heart! The officers came in after the man was finished praying and they put me back into the holding cell. Suddenly, a peace came over me that I could not understand.

I was then moved to a cell with a Mexican man who didn't greet me or say anything, he just stood there holding a bible for me to take. Saying nothing to him, I took the bible, threw it up on my bunk, and then tossed my bedding on top of it.

Over the next few days, finding I had nothing to do,

I began to look through that bible. When I told my mom about it she suggested I start reading the gospel of John, then Romans, and that's what I did. After several weeks, I wanted and even longed for, the peace the bible spoke of. The two things that I did not think even existed were love and peace. In my world, love was sex, "making love", and peace was someone else's world, certainly not mine.

I thought back to earlier times. When only eight, I was molested by a man whom I had never before met, and continued to be introduced to sexual things from the ages of ten to twelve; violently rejected by my biological father when I was ten, and kicked out of the house for a short period of time when I was twelve. Every man that I looked up to rejected and abandoned me.

I quit school in the eleventh grade, as well as, quitting every job I was ever given. I destroyed every relationship that I had with anyone. My entire attitude revolved around getting them before they got me; even toward the end of my freedom I walked into my own apartment with gun in hand to make sure that nobody was waiting there for me. I was addicted to cocaine and smoked about an ounce of weed a day. After destroying everything I touched, I was hopeless and tired of running. I needed and longed for a new life!

By reading those two books in the bible, I found hope that this 'God' just might be able to forgive me of all the horrible things that I did and had become. Longing for the two things which He offered, love and peace, I did the only thing that came to mind…I fell to my knees and asked Jesus to give me a new heart and life. Literally, like honey, the love and peace of God touched my head and ran all the way through my entire body and right into my feet. I broke!

I began to cry and cry and cry. I felt the urge to confess every single thing that I could think of. The powerful part of it was that I really wasn't confessing any of those things in order to be forgiven, but rather, to denounce the power that all those things had over my life.

About two hours later, as if a finalized work had occurred within me, I rose up a new man. I was different. I had become so hungry for God that all I did was feast upon the Word of the One who had somehow, supernaturally, transformed me. Within just a few days of giving my life to Jesus, I started to tell Him that I did not want to just say I loved Him and was His alone. Rather, I found myself telling Him, "God, I only know how to lie, but I want to prove my love to you. Please, God, show me something that I can do for you."

I started seeking what I could do for God. *What was this thing that was worthy enough to show Him how much I truly loved Him?* For about two weeks, I repeatedly sought this thing, this deed, for a sacrifice worthy enough to prove my love. Then, as I was reading the gospel of John I came to chapter 21, verses 15-19.

In the first three verses, Jesus was asking Peter, three different times, if he had loved Him. Each time, my own heart almost burst at the seams as I answered, "Yes, God! You know that I love you!" Then, I read verse 18 which says: "I am telling you the truth, when you were young, you used to get ready and go anywhere you wanted…" (*Thinking to myself, "Oh, God, you are right, you are speaking to me!*) "But when you are old, you will stretch out your hands and someone else will tie you up and take you where you don't want to go."

Everything within me burst and the only thing that I heard was God telling me, "Stop lying. Plead guilty to your part of the crime." *I get it!* The thing worthy enough to really show God how much I loved Him was to put my own life to death. In order to show God I loved Him and wanted to serve Him, that is what I set my heart to do…plead guilty to conspiracy to commit murder, which holds a natural life sentence without the possibility of parole.

As I hungered for God's Word, I ventured off into other books of the New Testament. It was then that God really revealed to me one of the most powerful scriptures that would form the rest of my walk and life in Him. "I write these things to you about those who are trying to deceive you. As for you, the anointing which you received from Him abides in you, and you have no need for anyone to teach you; but as His anointing teaches you about all things, and is true and is not a lie and just as it has taught you, you abide in Him." (1 John 2:26-27)

To me, back then, everything concerning the Word was life and was meant to be taken as the truth, the whole truth, and nothing but the truth, so help me God! While venturing into the Psalms (*my mom's suggestion*), I came across, "The words of the Lord are pure words; as silver tried in a furnace on the earth, refined seven times (Psalm 12:6). From that moment on, I believed that the Word of God was perfect and that there were no contradictions within it. I just believed that God through this anointing (*whom I know now is the Holy Spirit*) would teach me everything that I needed to know through His pure and perfect Word.

Later in my walk, I found myself beginning to find things within the Word that seemed to be contradicting itself within the scriptures, but I knew that it was not; it was just that I had not received the teaching (or revelation) of the anointing that would show me what it was actually saying, and not just what I was seeing as my own understanding. I began to tell the Holy Spirit, "Now I know that there are no contradictions within Your Word, but these scriptures appear to contradict themselves, so you will have to show me what is truly meant here so that I can have the spiritual understanding that properly interprets this verse." There were times that the Holy Spirit immediately gave me the understanding to see what was actually being spoken. Then there were other times where He brought me into the revelation of a scripture. Sometimes it took six months, or longer, before he would bring me back again to that original scripture, in order to give me the understanding. *Doing it this way finally made sense to me.*

I began to really cherish my reliance in the Holy Spirit, for how He would reveal so many things to me through these wonderful and marvelous revelations of the scriptures. God confirmed this process with two different verses. "Knowing this first that no prophecy of the scripture is of any private interpretation. For the prophecy came not in old time by the will of man: but holy men of God spoke as they were moved by the Holy Ghost." (2 Peter 1:20-21) And, "Eye has not seen, nor ear heard, neither have entered into the heart of man, the things which God has prepared for them that love Him. But God has revealed them unto us by His Spirit." (1 Corinthians 2:9-10a)

I learned that the truth of scripture never came from or through the will (or understanding) of man in the first place, *so of course, it could not come through man's own understanding of it now,* but revealed through the Holy Spirit. If the Word of God never changes, then the means in which He reveals Himself and what He has for those who love Him, can never change either. *God, the Holy 'Spirit, has so wonderfully opened my eyes throughout the years to these truths in which God has for us. How little I knew at the time that the scriptures would so powerfully form and shape me to be the man I am today, both in my own life, and in my ministry to His church.*

There was another really cool thing which happened during the time I was trying to find the sacrifice worthy enough to prove my love to Jesus. A black man was there with me. At first, he was in another cell, but in the same pod. I would talk with him and he would encourage me on my growth in the Lord. He was the first person I told what I had actually done in the committed crime.

The second person I told was the chaplain. Since I didn't want to tell my mom anything over the phone, I asked him to personally tell her. Not only did that help release something within me, but God used that to turn many hearts who were in the administration toward the possibility of witnessing the power of God in a criminal's life.

Shortly after that, both the black man and I were moved to another pod but put into the same cell. That guy was awesome! He would look up at the ceiling as if it wasn't even there, speaking about what he saw and how the angels were rejoicing in and over my obedience. He was in the same cell all the way up to my trial date and into the next day, when I was baptized in the Lieutenant's office.

That was a powerful moment in my life. The day before, I had pled guilty to the part of the crime that I committed and it seemed as though there was a covering lifted from me. It was as if God placed the covering over my life that I might, through His strength, plead guilty. When back in my cell at the county jail, the covering was lifted when I realized for the first time what I had just done. Fear and doubt gripped me with the words, "What did you just do?" I cried until I could cry no more. A fresh and new anointing came upon me as if Jesus Himself came and embraced me with an assurance of His love and pleasure toward me for my obedience toward Him.

It was the next morning when the Lieutenant came to my cell door and told me that the pastor of the church (which happened to be his own, as well as, my mom's church,) was here to baptize me. While walking down the hall to his office, he told me, "This is unheard of, there has not been a baptism in over thirty years and there will probably never be one again!" (Praise God though, for I heard many years later, that the jail had begun doing baptisms on a regular basis. Hallelujah to Jesus!)

We walked into his office and upon entering I could see three men standing there. One of them was the old man who, at the beginning, prayed for me. Every one of us greeted each other with a hug and then we proceeded. They had brought with them water from the baptismal pool from their church. I placed my head over a big tub and the pastor poured the water over my head saying, "I baptize you in the name of the Father, the Son, and the Holy Spirit." Then the pastor looked directly at me and laying his hand upon my shoulder said, "We are sending you as a missionary of our church into the darkest places of the world where we ourselves cannot go." *What a powerful moment!*

The next day my cell mate, the black guy, went home. He left me his phone number. Days later, I had my mom call that number but it wasn't in service. Nothing could be found out about the guy, not in jail nor in the streets. *I truly believe that God sent an angel to be there with me throughout the whole process of surrendering my life fully and completely to Jesus.*

God had moved so powerfully there, and not just within the inmates (many of whom gave their lives to Jesus), but also lives within the administration. I could not really see the profound work that was being done as it was happening, but *looking back now it was a truly powerful work that God did within the jail, where Jesus found me and where I found Jesus; not just as my Savior, but much more... as my Lord.*

2

QUARANTINE

Four months later I was transferred from the county jail to prison to begin my "new life". Upon entering the grounds of the prison, I must have been so overwhelmed at the sight and the feeling of this taunting facility, that I left my bible (my very first and cherished bible) on the seat of the cop car. I was devastated, to say the least!

I put in a kite to the chaplain for a new bible and I received one. So happy! Well, until I started to read something called the King James Version. It didn't matter how hard I tried, I could not understand that thing! It might as well have been written in another language, and I literally tossed it behind me onto my bunk. Discouraged again!

A guy in a neighboring cell handed me a bible that I could actually read; a Free on the Inside NIV Bible. *Hallelujah! I can understand it!* I was back to being super, super hungry for God's Word. So much so, that I was reading 10 hours a day every day.

While reading the New Testament, I noticed quotes from Isaiah and Hosea. Since there were no cross references in my bible, I decided to look up those passages and find out what they were talking about. Within 70 days I found all of the Old Testament passages that were referenced in the New

Testament. Every single one!

I had to face some pretty overwhelming things within the first few days of being in prison. First, was the sight and noise of cell block 7; it was referred to as quarantine. I was led through two huge metal doors to the control center of this hive of cells. On each side of the large room there were 5 tiers with 50 cells on each tier. Each cell in the front and the back had open bars; and each cell had a toilet, bunk and a desk. In total, there were 500 open cells. After receiving my tier and cell number, I began walking the entire stretch of this massive hive of cells, and up 3 flights of stairs to get to my 3rd tier, and then back across the length of the tier to get to cell number 12.

The second thing I had to face was any and all shyness of being naked or being around others who were naked. Every other day, in order for us to take a shower, the entire tier was let out of the cells and we would walk down the entire length of the tier to a spacious, open room where there were approximately 10 to 15 shower heads on the wall. We would all get naked, cram into this big room, wait for a shower to open up, and soap ourselves while we waited to rinse off the water. As if that wasn't enough, standing around looking right at us, were men and women guards. Therefore, if I wanted a shower, all shyness had to be confronted and driven out.

While there, I discovered that God was doing other things within and through me. I found myself preaching to the neighbors across from me, and at times, to the entire 250 cells which reached 5 tiers high. I noticed that as I preached, multiple people on the other side of the room would hang onto their bars, listening earnestly to what I was saying. Amazing!

It was in quarantine that I had my first vision/trance and an encounter with the devil. One day, while sitting on my bunk, we had been locked down within our cells for 23 hours and I was brought into a vision which was this:

I was sitting on my bunk talking to an inmate who was standing on the tier outside of my cell, when I was picked up and slammed continuously against the cell wall. The inmate started to yell for the guards and for the door to be opened. Whatever was slamming me up against the wall was not able to be seen by the human eye. Then the entity started to hit me in my face. I started to yell at the entity saying over and over again, "You can kill my body, but you can't take my spirit!"

The door was opened and two guards came rushing into the cell to help me, even though they had no idea how to do that. The entity let me go and grabbed both of the guards. One of the guards was thrown down the tier by the entity. I got up from the floor and ran to the aide of the other helpless guard, and the entity grabbed me and threw both of us over the railing of the third floor.

While plunging downward, I began to pray for protection for both the guard and me. The guard and I each smashed into a table and we both stood up without a scratch. Then, in front of us, two tables were smashed like they were twigs, and there appeared a gigantic serpent (very long and about 5 feet thick). The guard turned white and ran. I somehow had a tremendous amount of courage and strength come over me. I started praying and calling out that the shoes of the gospel of peace be put on my feet; that the belt of truth be put on my waist; the breastplate of righteousness be put on my chest; the helmet of salvation be put on my head; the shield of faith be put on my left arm; and the sword of the Spirit be put in my right hand.

As I was claiming the armor of God, each piece appeared in its right place upon my body. Once equipped, I jumped up on one of the standing tables and leaped toward the serpent, slicing into its breast and loudly yelling scripture. I repeated that 3 more times, when the serpent lunged and bearing its fangs, struck me with its open mouth... I leaped to the left, then onto a table where I jumped off, plunging my sword through the head of the beast and killing it.

I remember coming out of that vision rather fearful within my spirit, for I had no idea what any of that meant. When the time came for our one hour out of the cell, I called my mom and told her about the vision. She began praising God saying that the vision was a great thing and that God had shown me that He had given me victory over the devil. Once again, even though I still had no idea what the vision had actually meant, her understanding of it brought a sense of peace within my soul. God, His Word, everything was all still brand new to me. The only things that I had a knowledge of was what I read from the Bible, and the few encounters that I still had out in the world, both with God and demonic forces.

I remember my first encounter with God. It was when I was about 10 or 12 years old, and it involved a pastor named Van. In hopes that God would help turn me from the path I was on, my mom brought my sister and me to church. Every week, after the sermon when the altar call was given, she would tell me to go up front. One Sunday, literally, just to shut her up, I went forward.

There were 6 of us, and starting at the opposite end of where I was standing, the pastor began laying his hand on the head of the person in front of him, and down they went. I thought it odd, but whatever! The pastor continued doing the same to the next person, and then the next, and the same thing happened. I remember thinking to myself, "Oh no; I'm not going down!" The moment came when this pastor stood in front of me, lifted his hand and I felt a touch on my head. Everything within me was tight and I fought against going down, but it made no difference...down I went! Immediately, I jumped up fuming mad. I believe that day was when I rejected God, for after that I became so wicked. Although, God never stopped chasing after me. Praise His name for His never surrendering love for us!

The other encounters were with demonic presences, one of which I will share. I was about 15 or 16 years old and living at my mom's house. My sister had already moved out, and I lived in the basement which had two separate rooms. The first room, I always ran past the opening of in order to get to my room which was at the end of the hallway. So that you will have a better understanding, I will explain a few things.

First, when stepped on, every stair going down to the basement would loudly creak. Secondly, outside of my room there was a light in the hallway which could always be seen through the inch wide space between the door and floor. So, one night when I was alone in the house, I had my music going, and all of a sudden, as if one stair was being stepped on, I heard a creaking noise. I didn't think much about it, so I continued whatever I was doing. Again, I heard it. This time, I turned my music way down, and sure enough, I heard what sounded like someone coming down the stairs. With each creak, an overwhelming dread came over me. Then the creaking stopped, and I knew that whatever it was, was in the hallway. All of a sudden, two shadows blocked the light under the door, it was someone's feet! (*I can't help but laugh, even kind of embarrassed to admit*) I was sitting on the bed and I threw the sheets over my head (as if that would protect me!) Several minutes later, I got the nerve to get up from the bed. I leaped to the door, swung it open, and there was nothing there. I checked the entire house, nobody was there!

3

LEVEL 4

Finally, the day came to get packed up to go to where I would stay, the actual prison. We pulled up and entered the parking lot of the Level 4 facility and waited in the control center to find out which would be my unit and room. Once I was given the information, I entered the compound and the first thing that I saw everywhere, were flowers. *What a sight!*

Quarantine had been desolate, but then I remembered what I had told the judge when he asked if I had any last words before sentencing. I said, "I'm ready to start my new life!" *Now, I feel and see it.*

Even though that came to a pretty short end, as I entered the unit and walked down the hallway, I found that there were no keys to any of the doors, no bars, and fully secluded 8' x 12' cells. The door opened in front of me and I entered into my cell and met my cellmate.

My new cellmate was a young, black man and very high strung. During the stay with him I found that over and over again, God tested my faith. *I'm reminded of the scripture, "Every branch in me that does not bear fruit, He takes away; and every branch that bears fruit, He prunes it, so that it may bear more fruit."* (John 15:2) That was exactly what God was doing with me.

I found that, even though he didn't walk in any kind of religious way, the young man was a Muslim. Through him, I was introduced to his teacher and leader, which ended up being a blessing. The leader of the Sunny Muslims would continually call me out to walk and he would bring a younger Muslim with him and we would debate the Bible. I became really good at it, but I also became prideful, as well; at times thinking, "Yeah, I really cut him up!" I viewed the Word as a sword and my little pocket bible as my dagger.

Yet again, one day when coming back from a really good debate which I thought I had won, I was telling myself what a great job I had done defending Jesus and the Christian faith. God interrupted my boasting with a simple statement that changed my life. He said, "Yes, you cut him up really good, but who got saved?" *I tell you*, I felt about 2" tall. I repented and began to draw back from those debates, but throughout those times I really got to know the Muslim teacher and some of the other Muslim men.

I had a completely different battle within my cell. I found that my cell mate was stealing from me. Also, when I would get on my knees to pray he would lean over me from his top bunk and flick my ears with his fingers. Frustrated, but desiring to walk and act in love, I told him that it was not my ears that he was flicking, but the Lord's.

I went through trial after trial with the young man, until one day he did what should never be done. While laying prostrate on my bunk with my face in my pillow praying and calling out to God, all of a sudden I felt something wet hit the back of my head. I put my hand over the spot and realized that he had spit on me while I was praying.

In instant anger, I stood up, went to the sink, and began washing off the spit. All the while, I was telling God that I was done and that if He did not do something by the time that I finished washing it off I was going to kill that man (not literally), but we were going to fight. By the time I lifted my head from over the sink, the cell door was broke open and my name was called over the PA system.

It was announced for me to come to the officer's desk. There I was told that I had to go over to the school. From the desk, I headed in the direction of the school, and as I was walking over there, God spoke and said, "They spit on me, too!"

Instantly, all anger left and I broke down before God. I returned to the cell, no longer with anger, but rather with a deep and more profound love for my cell mate. Praise God, within two weeks that young man had his head on my right shoulder, bawling his eyes out, and giving his life and heart to Jesus. Hallelujah! Within a week or two afterward, he moved out and into another room.

I found that I was preaching to anyone that wanted to walk and listen, and I acquired a pretty cool name, Preacher Man. Around that time, I lived with a middle aged guy that believed in Jesus, but he struggled to find release and freedom from a few things.

I was unaware that the man had a heroin addiction. I

should have known since he had told me that he always used to get high in abandoned buildings when he was on the outside. I found out later that once he became incarcerated, he began buying from someone on the yard and had built up quite a debt.

He had a bad knee but was assigned to the top bunk. It was difficult for him to jump up and out of his bed. We obtained permission to switch bunks so that he wouldn't have to put more strain on his knee.

The very next day, we received items from the store. Orders were placed on Sunday night and the people who worked in the store would bring the actual goods into our units on Thursday morning before we went to the yard. Afterward, yard was called and I got in line to take a shower. (At that facility, a one-man shower, a total of two showers for each floor within the unit. Four wings, or floors, thus eight showers total for the unit.) When I exited the shower, the door of our room was open and my cell mate was not in there.

As I entered the room, I discovered that all of my store goods that were received that morning were gone. Immediately, I was mad! There were only two ways the door could have been opened. Either my cell mate left it open and set me up to get robbed; or the officers at the front desk opened it for someone.

I ran out of the room and went outside to confront my cell mate. When I found him, out of anger, I started yelling that he had just set me up. He immediately said, "I did not;

I didn't leave the door open." By that time, we had the attention of everyone on the yard. I just left and went back into the cell, closed the door, and fell on my knees. I began asking forgiveness for my outburst of anger, and asked God to forgive my Bunkie and whoever else may have been involved.

I felt broken that I had placed cans of tobacco and a couple of other things before God. By the time I finished praying, my cell mate was there begging me to believe him that he had nothing to do with the theft.

That afternoon the Grand Sheik of the Muslim community took it upon himself to resolve the issue. *Now here is the manifested power of God!* What had happened was, the heroin dealer thought that my Bunkie still slept on the top bunk, and thinking the store items were his, they mistakenly took what was really mine. They had used the laundry man to have the officers open the cell door.

The Muslims found out who was involved, and told two of the three, to lock up, or they were going to get holes put in them (stabbed with homemade knives, called shanks). And as if that wasn't enough, later that night, the Grand Sheik had two pouches of cigarettes slid under my door *(that's unheard of!) Just pointing out, because I was quick to forgive and asked forgiveness, God used the ungodly to bring wrath to the ones who stole from me. He even gave me a few smokes that would get me to the next store! He, so wonderfully, showed me that He will always have my back, and that the wicked one will not get away with touching His anointed one. Praise God!*

It wasn't long before the ones on the yard were beginning to mock me for smoking cigarettes. They would put two fingers together bringing them to their mouths, and say, "Hallelujah, oh hallelujah to Jesus!" At first, I didn't understand where this was coming from, *but now I really do praise God for it.*

While I was in the county jail, I wasn't tempted and had no desire because there was no smoking allowed there. However, once I got into quarantine, there was a window for every five cells. Since I had a window in mine, all the smoke from everyone would be drawn to the window. Without fail, so it seemed, a small wind would blow through and the smoke drifted directly into my cell.

The first couple of nights, I hacked and almost choked on the smoke, so I did what anyone still weak in their faith would do. *If I can't beat them I'll join them!* Once again, I picked up the habit.

I set my heart on quitting smoking. In fact, I must have tried at least 20 times. Over and over again, I would put them down and then pick them right back up. One day, while reading the book of Romans in my bible, *I love the book of Romans*, I read, "And if you are sure that you yourself are a guide to the blind, a light to those who are in darkness, an instructor of the foolish, a teacher of children, having in the law the embodiment of knowledge and truth – you then who teach others, do you not teach yourself? While you preach against stealing, do you steal? You who say that one must not commit adultery, do you commit adultery? You who boast in the law dishonor God by breaking the law. For as it is written, "The name of God is blasphemed among the Gentiles because of you." (Romans 2:19-21)

My heart sank and I was broken! *Right here, right now, I am the one who is blaspheming God among the Gentiles.* I began asking God how to be delivered from smoking, and ultimately blaspheming His name. He brought me to the book of Isaiah, the chapter on fasting. "Is not this the fast that I choose: to loosen the bonds of wickedness, to undo the bands of the yoke, to let the oppressed go free, and that you break every yoke?" (Isaiah 58:6)

Within my heart, I shouted, "Yes, yes, yes…it is God who does it!" Then I asked Him how many days, and He gave me the words Jesus spoke, "They have now been with me for three days, and have had nothing to eat." (Mark 8:2) *Now I know what to do and how many days.* I started the very next day. I didn't fast from smoking, but from eating!

And, I smoked like a chimney! We had cans of bugler back then and I, literally, smoked ¾ of a can within those three days. For God never told me to stop smoking for three days, but to stop eating, which is the definition of a fast! At least, that is what I was telling myself at the time.

On the fourth morning, I woke up and when the officers called my wing of the unit, I went to chow. Upon stepping outside the door of the unit a guy in front of me lit up a cigarette, and a puff of smoke came right into my face. I almost vomited. It was the most disgusting thing, as if I had never before smoked. I never picked up another one.

One time a guy handed me a cigarette to hold for a moment; he turned around and before he turned back for his smoke, I had already broken it in half and threw it away. Needless to say, he never again handed me a smoke. I had an uncompromising faith that if God delivered me from smoking then I would not hold nor give to anyone else a smoke. Even when a brother, feigning for one, asked if he could get a stamp (our currency back then), I told him, no, for I knew that he was going to buy smokes with it. Since God had delivered me, no way was I going to provide cigarettes to anyone else.

Well, he got in the flesh and became very angry. One day when I was walking the yard with a few friends, I got hit with a basketball. At the time, I didn't think anything of it for the ball goes everywhere when people are playing basketball. After I was hit again, I saw that the same brother who asked for a stamp for some smokes was the one who was throwing the ball. Harder and harder he began throwing it, and I was getting madder by the minute!

The Spirit of God spoke to me and said, "If you let a spirit back in, you will become seven times worse than before!" I could not imagine myself worse than I was before, and in an instant, an anointing came upon me. I started to rejoice and shout very loudly, "HALLELUJAH!" Each and every time that the dude hit me with a basketball, I shouted praises to God. I even caught the ball once and actually rolled it back to the guy! *God is amazing!*

A few days later as chow was about to begin, I was overcome with fear when the guy who had been hitting me with the ball said he wanted to talk to me. I really didn't want to get into a fight. I had to walk right past the guy's cell in order to get off the wing, but I bound the fear and went forward. The guy came out and began to walk right next to me but didn't say anything until we got outside.

All of a sudden, the guy began crying and asking me to forgive him for what he had done to me. My spirit broke; I just grabbed him and hugged him. I told him that I still loved him and that he was most certainly forgiven. A few weeks later he got packed and moved over to Level 2. A couple of months passed and I was in the weight pit working out when I heard someone far away shouting, "Anthony! Anthony!" I looked up and realized that the same brother, who had months earlier tried to coax me into a fight, was now shouting my name just to tell me, "God bless you and thank you! *How amazing to us is our God?*

A short time after that, I was working as a third shift porter. I finished cleaning the showers and returned to my cell. I began flipping through channels of the TV and found an Evangelistic movie that was just starting on one of the Christian stations, and began watching it.

By the end of that movie, I just broke down and started to weep. I held my chest and began asking God to forgive me of anything that I might have done to sin against Him. As I was worshipping and crying out to Him, suddenly there was a fear that entered the room which I have never before experienced. I was frozen in fear, not dread but fear. All of a sudden it lifted and the glory of God filled the room. It was amazing! The presence became stronger and stronger. At one point, I sat up in my bunk with my legs hanging off the side, and waved my right hand in front of me. It, literally, felt like I was waving my hand through thick water; His presence was that thick! I was laughing and praising Him. Mind you, it was about 2:00 in the morning. It became more and more intense and tangible to me that at one point, I actually thought the ceiling was going to be ripped off and Jesus was going to be standing there! It was an encounter I will NEVER forget and I strive to, once again, get back to that place within my life and ministry.

During that time I would read nothing but the Bible. There were many people who would ask if I wanted to read this book or another, but I would always tell them the same thing, "Nope, thank you, but I'm reading 66 books right now!" (There are 66 books in the Bible.)

One cell mate, however, came back from the chaplain's library with a book which he said I needed to read. Of course, as always, I told him the same thing, but he stressed the point that I would love the book. With over 800 pages, it was a big ole' thing titled, "Smith Wigglesworth: The Complete Collection of His Life Teachings".

This time, something was a bit different within me. A peace came over me concerning that book. So, I took it and began reading the author's first sermon. Wow! Everything I had read from the Bible began to unfold right before my eyes and within my heart. The same anointing I had felt when reading the Bible was very present. The authority which the people said Jesus had was the same authority I was experiencing while reading Wigglesworth's book. A new world opened up to me.

The author showed me a revelation for everything that Jesus and His disciples did. *To myself, I think: as the Holy Spirit brings scripture after scripture to mind about what Jesus, Paul, and Peter said about us doing the same things that Jesus had done NOW, TODAY!* So this was the first person that God opened my heart to and I feasted!

I began reading about others, in our present day (i.e. Kenneth E. Hagin and Kenneth Copeland), who were speaking and performing supernatural things of God. I started to see a connection though, not just in Spirit and the authority of their words, but in which translation of the bible that all of them were quoting from...The King James Version. *Is this not the same bible that I threw on the bed because I could not understand it? What is up with this translation?* So, I called home and asked my mom to send me a "plain Jane" King James Version. At that point I had probably gone through 50 study bibles, of different translations, but I always stayed away from the KJV because I could not understand it.

Once I received my plain KJV, something awesome began happening as I started to read from the New Covenant. It was as if my eyes were opened and I could somehow understand that Bible. For whatever reason, there was a complete difference from my first experience with this translation. I found I was growing so much in my dependence to the Holy Spirit, the translation revealed what things meant. Needless to say, I found my translation to which I have stuck to ever since.

There was one point in time where I began asking God to reveal to me my calling. While seeking God's answer, I went out to the big yard (which is just a bigger yard than the regular, small fenced in yard which was in front of the units.) I was sitting on a picnic table with a couple of brothers, just fellowshipping, when God brought me back into remembrance of what the head pastor had said after he baptized me. "We send you into the darkest places of the earth, where we ourselves cannot go, as a missionary of our church." As soon as I saw that, I heard a word, it was almost audible…Evangelist. *"Yes, that's it; I'm an Evangelist!"* From that moment on, I just believed that was my calling.

One Sunday morning I got ready and went to church. When I got there, the regular volunteer wasn't there, but instead, there were three black women (guessing they were around 40 years old). They were pretty awesome. At the end of the service, they were handing out sheets of paper to each of us. It was a prophecy given by some man named Bill. I took it, folded it in half and put it in my bible. Back at the cell later that day, I pulled the piece of paper out and read the prophecy.

Here is what I read:

"It was late and I was tired. I wanted to go to sleep,

but God was wanting to talk. It was about midnight when it dawned on me…God does not sleep. His question made me restless: "Bill, where on earth does man keep his most priceless treasures and valuables?" I said, "Lord, usually treasures, like gold, silver, diamonds, and precious jewels, are kept out of sight, usually with guards and security, under lock and key."

God spoke: "My most valuable treasures on earth are also kept locked." Then I saw Jesus standing in front of, seemingly, thousands of jail cells. The Lord said, "These have almost been destroyed by the enemy, but have the greatest potential to be used to bring forth glory to my name. Tell my people, I am going this hour to the prisons to activate the gifts and callings that lie dormant in these lives that were given before the foundations of the earth. Out from these walls will come forth an army of spiritual giants who will have power to, literally, kick down the gates of hell and overcome satanic powers that are holding many of my own people bound in my own house. Tell my people that great treasures are behind these walls in these forgotten vessels. My people must come forth and touch these, for a mighty anointing will be unleashed upon these for future victory in my kingdom. THEY MUST BE RESTORED!"

Then, I saw the Lord step up to the cells holding a key that fit every lock, and the doors began to open. I saw a great explosion, as if dynamite had been detonated behind the prison walls, it sounded like all out spiritual warfare. Jesus turned and said, "Tell my people to come in now and pick up the spoils and rescue these." He walked in and touched inmates who were clinging to him. After he touched them, they immediately glowed. Some had golden, others a silver glow, to which God said, and "There is my gold and silver!"

As if in slow motion, they began appearing as giant knights wearing armor. Like warriors, they had on the full armor of God and every piece was pure, solid gold, they even held golden shields. I heard God say to these warriors, "Now go, take what Satan taught you and use it against him. Pull down the strongholds which are coming against my church!"

The spirited giants then started stepping over the prison walls. Nobody resisted them and they went immediately to the front lines of battle against the enemy. Like David going after Goliath, I saw them walk right past the churches and big named ministers who were known for their power with God. Demons flew out of sight at their presence, as they crossed over enemy lines and started delivering many of God's people from the clutches of Satan.

No one, seemed to know who these spirited giants were or where they came from, not even the church. All you could see from head to toe was the golden armor of God. The shields of gold were being restored to God's house and there was great victory and rejoicing. Also, being brought in were diamonds, precious jewels, and vessels. Those valuables were the people that nobody knew. **Rejects of society, street people, outcasts, the poor and despised, were among the treasures that were missing from His house.**

In closing, the Lord said, "If My people want to know where they are needed, tell them they are needed in the streets, the hospitals, the missions, and the prisons."

Talk about getting excited about something! I saw myself in every word I was reading.

After being in Level 4 for two years, I believed that I would be there for 4 to 6 more years before I could go to Level 2. Imagine my surprise when I was called to the desk one morning and told, "Pack your property, you're going to Level 2." To the officer, I shouted, "What? Hallelujah!"

God had given me so much favor with the staff that they were wavering me, 4 years early, to the Level 2 side of the compound!

4

LEVEL 2

With all my belongings, I entered the unit. While walking through the yard I heard one person after another yelling my name and they began running toward me. There were so many people whom I knew and had ministered to from Level 4. It seemed as if they were coming out of the wood work!

Within that first two weeks of being in Level 2, I had never before in my life had so many embraces, or received so much love from people. I found that not just the attitudes of the people were completely different, but the entire atmosphere was just brighter. The Sunday morning services were awesome! The Spirit of God was so much more present in those services than when in Level 4. I loved it!

I quickly fit in with the already established leadership there and I found myself growing differently than when in Level 4, quarantine or the county jail. Prior to that, my time had been spent in the Word, but I didn't have a big prayer life. Level 2 was different, God was working on and through my ministry of serving and witnessing to others more than ever before, which in turn drove me into an actual prayer life.

After six months or so of being there, I was in a cell with

an older man who wasn't a believer, but I knew he really respected my faith. One day he was packed up and sent away from the facility; then God, literally made that cell into a transitional room.

In that cell I witnessed to 21 different bunkies within a 30-day period, twenty- one! To others, there was just no desire at all to even speak with them. I became aware that it wasn't about telling everyone about Jesus, but rather telling those who God wanted a seed planted, or to water what was already within them. For, "No man can come to me, except the Father who has sent me draws him..." (John 6:44)

I began to see and learn how the Spirit works. My dependence on what the Spirit was doing, and wanted to do, was amazing to me! I observed Him doing this or that with one person yet he provided no work or anything else for another. I started to understand the scriptures which told about Paul's ministering to others that they "were forbidden of the Holy Ghost to preach the Word in Asia". After they came to Mysia, they assayed (left) to go into Bithynia; but the Spirit did not permit them". (Acts 16:6-7) It amazed me that the Spirit would powerfully enable me to minister to some, but not to others.

That brought me to my first struggle with the principle of the law. Previously, I had been so hungry for the Word of God, but all I was doing was focusing on ministering to others, and that severely limited my own time in the Word. With that came the guilt of not reading as much as I used to do. So, I began to set an amount of chapters, not hours, to read each day.

I'm not sure how I came up with 25 chapters, but that was the number that I set for myself. As you can probably guess, yes, I fell short time after time which brought on even more guilt. I often condemned and convinced myself that I was not living up to the standard that I thought I had to live up to for Him to love and be pleased with me.

One day, I found myself asking forgiveness for not reading enough pages. The Spirit brought me into the remembrance of a scripture, "...and the strength of sin is the law." (1 Corinthians 15:56) He began to show me that, "Christ is the end of the law for righteousness to everyone that believes". (Romans 10:4) For the law is always about do not do this, or that, and the Holy Spirit was showing me that I was doing the exact same thing to myself. I was bringing myself under the law by saying, "Do not read anything less than 25 chapters a day." So I was actually strengthening sin within me by setting a law over myself instead of accepting that what God was doing within and through me as enough.

Yes, faith without works is dead, but "the law is not of faith..." (Galatians 3:12) and "without faith it is impossible to please God." (Hebrews 11:6) I had been forcing myself to live up to an anointing that God had given me for a period of time within my life. Rather than walking by the leading of the Spirit and trusting that He knew what was best for me, I was, in actuality, fighting against God. He said, "...I will do a new thing, and it will come to pass." (Isaiah 43:19) However, rather than relying on His leadership, I was still trying to do what had become my comfortable way of life.

During my stay in Level 2, God really began to sharpen my prayer life. The scripture that would come to mind continually was, "Can you not pray for one hour?" (Matthew 26:40) I consistently forced myself to pray longer, to stay there. I began to praise Him and focus on how He was ministering within me. I found that the more I did that the longer I was in prayer without having to force myself.

One of the big things was my relationship with Him, trusting that His word would dig deep within my heart and produce a wild fire within me. The more I prayed like that, the more I found that God was giving me opportunities with others on the yard, and He was revealing Himself to us. It was awesome! My prayers were lasting from thirty minutes to an hour, then two, and at times even three hours. I was just feasting with His Spirit in my prayer life.

One day a buddy and I were sitting outside on the picnic table. A guy began running around the outer perimeter, and all on the yard could hear him loudly swearing, as he cursed the name of Jesus. Time after time he came by our table, and when I would hear him I bound that wicked spirit, but the man continued cursing. My spirit was so grieved that no matter how much I bound that spirit within that man he just continued swearing.

I returned to my room and got on my knees. While remembering God's Word about the authority that He had given unto us, I prayed. I was so ashamed that I had not been in a place of the Spirit when that devil came out, and my prayers began to change. I found myself asking God to show me His glory and to allow it to fall down upon me. That became my focus, and the desire for that began to grow deep within me.

While asking for His glory to be revealed, I began to pray in tongues, intense praying, and at times lasting nine hours. Just as Eli asked God to show His glory, I found myself in what I call a season of prayer. Each and every night I was praying for at least three, sometimes six hours at a time.

There were so many revelations, battles, and visions during that season of seeking His glory. I remember one time when I was brought into a vision while in prayer. I saw a little girl who wore a pink dress and she had long, blond hair. At first, her back was to me, but then she began to turn and face me. As she did, her face turned almost demonic and she pulled out a knife and stabbed me right in the chest. I awoke from the vision, literally, grabbing my chest. The entire room was filled with a dark, tangible presence. I immediately bound that spirit with the name of Jesus and the entire room's atmosphere changed. Again, peace settled over me.

Another time during that season of praying, I had an urge to telephone my mom and she was so glad I called. She told me my cousin, who lived in Texas, was in need of prayer. She was in the hospital with a rare, Japanese virus. I climbed on my bunk, got on my knees, and began to pray. Within about an hour, I was brought into a vision whereby I entered my cousin's hospital room. I walked around her bed and I laid my left hand upon her head and my right hand upon her stomach. I commanded the illness to come out of her. I saw her sit up from the bed, healed.

The following week, I called my mom, having not talked to her since she asked me to pray. She answered with joy in her voice and shared the good news. My cousin was out of the hospital, fully healed. Hallelujah to Jesus!

There was another time when I called my mom at home, and she told me that my dad (stepdad) was in the hospital for heart problems, and that everything was just not going their way. One of the nurses had been rude, he had been given the wrong medication (even after my mom told them he was allergic to it), and another nurse had carelessly pulled out a tube that went from his neck to his heart. One thing after another had my mom at her wit's end. So, we prayed over the phone and I loosed the angels to surround them.

Later, when my mom returned to the hospital, the first thing my dad said to her was, "Do you see them?"

"See who?"

My dad, matter-of-factly, answered, "The angels that are standing at the door."

My mom told me after that there was a completely different feeling in that room. Hallelujah to Jesus!

God also brought me through many trials. There was an older man who was not a believer, but knew the scriptures. He did everything he could to get me off my square. Directly next to my bed was a bulletin board where he placed some nude pictures of women, I could see them all the time. I noticed that at the bottom of each picture were printed the women's names. I began to pray out loud for these women and would call them by name each and every one of them, praying for their salvation and deliverance from the spirit of lust that was in them. Within two days after starting that I walked into the room and all the pictures were gone from the bulletin board. Hallelujah to Jesus! Victory! Some years later, I saw that same man at another facility. He came up to me and asked if I remembered him. I said I did, and I asked how he was doing. He told me that he wanted to thank me. He said God had used me as the example for him to come to know Jesus as His Lord and Savior. Again and again, hallelujah!

While at Level 2, God laid a forty year old man with mental and physical problems on my heart, and as I began helping him, he just clung to me. I found that he wouldn't listen to anybody else, but he would listen to me. God, so wonderfully, gave me much grace and love toward the man. He used me to teach that man the most basic things in life.

That man, no matter what he was eating, would use his fingers. I taught him to use a fork and spoon, and how to brush his teeth, for he had never done those things. We take so many things for granted, but that man had little knowledge, I even had to tell him to wipe himself after going to the bathroom.

The staff really took notice of that and once the man

rode out I asked to be moved in with a deaf guy, who was also in his forties, but had the mindset of a twelve year old. They quickly put me in with him and a noticeable change began to occur within the man. He knew that I had requested to be moved in with him and he just started responding to the staff and others in the unit. One day, the officers called me to the desk and told me to move to another room. Because I was moved, the deaf man, unfortunately, flipped out, lost his temper, and got into a fist fight with one of the officers.

There was something funny that happened when they told me to move. I was moved in with an older man, around 60, who was in a wheel chair. I had just started moving my things into his room and he immediately wheeled himself to the door frame and started to yell up to the officers. "I know why you are moving him into my room! He can't save me!" Then he glared at me and said, "You can't save me!" Over and over again he was yelling that at the top of his lungs! Talk about a powerful witness, I hadn't even said a word to the man. Throughout my stay in that room he didn't give his life to the Lord, but I know that the discussions we had over the Word of God really softened his heart toward me and toward Jesus.

The most trying and yet the most beautiful thing that happened to me at Level 2 was when God had given me a word to speak over the church concerning their worldly condition. I went to the elder and asked him for a few minutes to give this word. After revealing to him what God had given me, he told me that God gave the same message a few years ago through another man, and he granted me permission to speak.

When that Sunday came, I was quite nervous, but as I started to speak the Spirit wonderfully took over and afterward He led me to say what Paul had spoken in the scriptures, "To those who will not yield and change that they would be delivered over to Satan for the destruction of the flesh, that their spirit may be saved in the day of the Lord Jesus." (1 Corinthians 5:5) Then I gave an altar call and six men came up and we prayed.

I thought that it had been a success until later that afternoon. To my surprise, one of the people who were looked to as a leader came up and told me that I had to repent. He claimed that what I had said was not of God. I told him that it was and that I would not repent. From then on, not only the church, but people who weren't even believers began attacking me verbally. It was interesting to find out that a few years later that same leader who had accused me of false prophesying didn't even believe that Jesus was part of the Godhead. However, the elder to whom I went for permission never said anything negative to me. That happened all week long and I was getting weak from defending that which was given by God.

The following Saturday we had a worship service that lasted two hours. As usual, I would always go to the back of the room and just pray throughout the services for God to move. A volunteer came in, who was usually very in tune with what the Spirit was doing. I wasn't sure if some of the people there told him that I was falsely prophesying or what,

46

but the man said that about two hours before he came in, the Spirit told him that someone was causing a lot of strife within the church and that the person was not of God.

I broke down! I'd had it. After the service I left and went to my cell. Another brother with whom I was very close, who had been encouraging me the prior week, came to the door. I took my prayer box and shoved it into the dear brother's chest, telling him I was done! *I'm done with it all!* I got on my knees and just wept before God asking, "Why?" I received no answer, but I knew that God had given me that word!

The following morning, the same brother who had encouraged me, came and asked to walk with me before the church service; although, I was bound and determined not to go. That dear brother and I talked and he told me to give God one more chance. He said for me to go and if God didn't do anything to defend me or to answer me then fine, just for me to stop going, but he urged me to not give up on God.

So, I went; but I talked to no one. I just walked directly to my corner in the back of the room where I always prayed, got on my knees and started to pray. The brother who had come in from the outside gave a message that was pretty much hitting everything that God had told me to speak the week before. At the end of the service, the invitation was given for anyone who wanted to rededicate or give their life to Jesus. I heard a little movement, then the volunteer asked again, this time saying, "I know there are more than this, seriously guys we need to be and get right with God!"

A few seconds after that, God told me to look up. *In*

my *"righteous"* anger... *"Nope! Not doing it!"* Again, he told me to look up, my answer was still the same. For the third time He once again told me the same thing, I knew God wasn't going to give up, so I humbled myself and looked up. *What a sight to behold!*

Every single person was on their knees in front of their chairs giving their lives to Jesus, all but one man in the very back, last row, about 5 feet from me to my right. He looked over at me, nodded his head, and then looked back up front. My face just hit the floor in praise and repentance!

After that service, I tried to find that man for I had never before seen him. I couldn't find him anywhere, and no one else knew who I was even talking about! Hallelujah, Jesus had sent an angel to defend me! Not one person came and asked for forgiveness for calling me a liar or a false prophet, but the thought that everyone was on their faces before God was more than I could have ever asked for or even possibly thought. *Amazing is our God!* There were a few brothers though who began to call me a prophet, but I gently corrected them and told them that I was an evangelist and not a prophet.

While in Level 2 I had a few people who would just stop in, sit down in my room, and we would talk about the scriptures. One day there was a Mexican man who stopped at my door and asked for prayer about something, so we prayed. After that, he began to stop in occasionally, would sit down, and I would just share the Word with him that God had placed on my heart. That went on for a few weeks.

Another guy told me that the Mexican man was a hit

man for the Mexican Cartel. Whether that was true or not, it really didn't matter much to me. Even after I heard that, whenever he would stop by I would just speak the Word over his life. One day he came into my room and there was something different about him, there was even a difference in the atmosphere, but I just thought he was having a bad day *which is very easy to have in prison.* I just brushed it off and as he sat down I began to minister and tried to encourage him in the things of God.

All of a sudden, he abruptly stopped me in mid-sentence, stood up and left the room. I wondered what that was all about, for there had been no explanation or "excuse me", or anything. So, I said a quick word of prayer for him and went about my day. A few days later, he again showed up. That time there was a more peaceful presence about him. He started out the talk that day with something I never saw coming.

The man said, "You know the last time I was here, I came in with three shanks (homemade knives); I was going to kill you!" (I thought to myself: Wow! Really dude? Yet, at the same time I was praising God.) The man continued to say that he was going to do it, but then something, out of nowhere, stopped him, which he could not understand nor explain, and it drove him out of the room. Oh, Hallelujah to Jesus for His mighty angels who are always with us when we are going about our Father's business! *So powerful is God!* It was that day, I was given the scripture *which I still continue to stand on,* "Touch not mine anointed, and do my prophet no harm." (Psalm 105:15)

Toward the end of my three year stay at Level 2, God brought me into a vision where He showed me going to three different prisons, all of them being the worst in the state. I shared that vision with the church and others. I was very excited about it for I thought I was ready for whatever would be thrown at me, and that I was willing to do anything that God told me.

One day I was working as the chaplain's clerk and the Classification Director came over to me and asked if I wanted to go to another facility (one I had seen in my vision), for he knew that I was trying to get a transfer. I told him I needed to pray about it. Once I got the "Go forth" from God, I told the Director, "Yes." I was so excited about going to where God had shown me.

Shortly thereafter, the day came when the officers called me to the desk and told me to pack up for I was transferring. Hallelujah! My adventure was beginning! (Or, so I thought!)

5

MY FIRST TRANSFER

The day had come to start the adventure of going into what God had shown me... one of the worst three prisons in the state. Before leaving Level 2, the officers did the usual strip search to make sure we had nothing on us but our paperwork. I always carried my pocket bible on me everywhere I went. Bless God for He had given me favor with the officer; he allowed me to keep my bible.

All day long we travelled from facility to facility dropping off people and picking up people. All the while I was reading The New Testament from my pocket bible. We ended up dropping off the last two guys, besides myself, I found myself left alone as we were about to arrive at my new location. What a blessing I received! It was then night time and the officers turned on the lights within the entire length of the bus just so I could read my bible. Favor!

At the prison, the next day I went to pick up my property, for the officers had to go through it and remove anything that wasn't allowed. After I retrieved my belongings, I was walking back to my unit, and a man yelled out from the other side of the yard. "How many of you came in last night?"

"Just me." I shouted back. Immediately, the Spirit spoke to me and said, "No, four of you came in." *Yes, you are right,*

Lord, the Father, the Son and the Holy Spirit came in with me! Hallelujah to Jesus!

I found out a few things about the new place. The chaplain was from a stout Catholic background and kept a very strong hand upon the protestant services. I was told by other believers that the man would yell, even curse, at some of the volunteers if they preached on anything of which he didn't approve. Even when I prayed with the volunteers before they spoke at a service, they would continually look over at the chaplain, as if to make sure he approved of me praying over them. *Crazy is what that was!* He and I just didn't see eye to eye!

During the Christmas season that year, around midnight, while lying on my bunk, I was praying, at which time the Holy Spirit said, "Ask and I will show you the sorrows of my heart." My response was, "No way! I don't want to know what makes your heart sorrowful, I can only imagine. *Nope, not doing it.*" Again, He spoke, "Ask and I will show you the sorrows of my heart." *Nope, sorry can't do that.* He repeated his original statement. Again, I knew He was not going to stop until I was obedient, so I very cautiously said to Him, "Lord, show me the sorrows of your heart. *Do I even dare to ask? Yes Lord, show me your sorrows.*" Immediately I was brought into a vision which was:

I saw myself in Thailand and a Tsunami was coming and was visible. I started to walk toward the water when my wife pulled on my arm begging me to run from it with her. I cried, "Let go of me!" She grabbed her child and began weeping as she ran. I walked about 5 feet or so into the water and called out, "I command you Tsunami, peace be still in Jesus name!" I shut my eyes in complete silence when a tiny wave hit my feet ever so gently. Upon opening my eyes, I found that just a couple of minutes before, the wave had been a massive Tsunami.

Within some minutes, my wife came running up to me, fell on her knees and cried out, "I'm not worthy, forgive me!" I told her, "The grace and mercy of the Lord is upon you, my dear wife. If God is for us, who or what can be against us? For there is no weapon formed against us that shall prosper."

The Lord then brought me out of the vision and began to open the eyes of my heart saying, "The wife is my sorrow!" (Knowing in my heart that the wife is the body of Christ, running in fear instead of believing, acting and speaking in His name.) That was a huge eye opener to me, but I saw it. So many people claim to know Christ Jesus, and yet don't believe what He said He would do through his church, through all the ages. My heart broke in realizing that the traditions of man has made void the power of God from their lives.

I spent another month or so in that unit, and then moved to the non-smoking section which was established for us. There was a man there named Alex who was known throughout the system for being a clerk and tutor at other facilities. *I share that because the chaplain refused to hire a clerk.* We found out that the chaplain was placed on disciplinary leave for 6 weeks because he kept leaving his radio all over the place, which was a security issue.

While the chaplain was gone, the facility hired Alex, based on his clerical skills. His duties were to do all the religious sign-in sheets and whatever else needed to be done in that capacity. God gave that man, as well as myself, favor with the officer who ran the building, wherein we had all of our religious and worship call out (which we created). A lot of people came and, WOW, did God move! Everyone was involved. The services consisted of singular and corporate singing, prophesying, Spirit-lead prayers, and physical and emotional healing. It was powerful.

After six weeks, the chaplain returned to work. He was furious with the facility for hiring a clerk, and on his first day back, just because a call had been created which he couldn't control, he fired Alex. From that moment on the chaplain and I were always at odds. He was more verbal, but I knew that it was spiritual.

Out on the yard, God had begun to really move. People would come up to Alex and me, seeking prayer for all sorts of things; our prayers would continuously be answered. Many gave their lives to Jesus, others grew stronger in their relationship with Him, but all knew that God was moving in mighty ways.

For a period of time I worked in the kitchen, first on the line serving food, and then delivering trays to the units. When going through the hallways of the mental health unit, I began seeing signs hanging on cell doors. One read, "Coping with voices". My heart broke as I read that and so from then on, each time I would pass those doors, I would pray against those demonic voices, that those people would break free from coping and gain victory over the voices.

The kitchen staff started having me come in at 4:30 a.m. to set up the food trays. It was wearing me down. I found that when I got back to my cell, around 2:00 p.m., all I wanted to do was sleep. I didn't have the drive for ministry because I was just too tired. As I was in prayer about that, I started to ask God what to do. I told Him that I would rather have no money and all of Him, rather than some money and none of Him. *I need more of Him!* No, I needed all of Him and I couldn't get my spiritual needs met with that job.

I decided that I was going to quit. Policy stated that if I did so before six months, I would be on double 0 status, which is being locked down in my room from 6 a.m. until 4 p.m. Based on the fact that I needed all of God in my life, I went in to work that morning determined to quit my job. When I arrived I found that the regular staff was not there, but staff from another shift. So, I told the food steward that I was quitting. The man knew how much of a good worker I was, although he only recognized the work done rather than the One for whom I truly worked. He tried to talk me out of it, but I was done.

For the steward's sake, I finished the day out, and the very next day I began my two days off. During those two days no one wanted to write me the ticket which would put me on double 0 status. I knew it was God's hand all over it.

When it was time for me to return to work, I did not go in and they called me out. The main steward was mad because the time line for writing a ticket on me had passed. Praise God I was able to walk out with no consequences of any kind. Again, Hallelujah to Jesus!

Between the hard feelings I'd had toward the chaplain and escaping the kitchen situation, I was told to pack up my property for I was being transferred. The following day I was told to get on the bus for my transfer out of there. I looked back as the bus pulled away, shook the dust off my feet, and cursed that place because of their hardened hearts toward God and His gospel.

6

THE DARK PLACE

After the six hour drive, we pulled up to the northern facility, the dark place. After being told where my bunk was I placed the few things I was carrying down and waited for the next day to retrieve the rest of my property.

I left the building and went out to the yard, and what a yard it was! Huge! It had a mile running track which circled the entire yard. Trees everywhere! There were three spacious lots for gardening, and two baseball fields. A large weight pit was all open which meant that anyone could go and lift weights anytime they wanted. Every other place I had been, the weight pit was enclosed with fences and could only be used through the call-out system.

One of the first things I was told by an inmate was, "I hope you like the cold because here we have winter 8 months of the year!" He was right!

Spiritually speaking it seemed like everything there was thriving. Throughout the first few months, I found there were religious call outs for Baptist, Assembly of God and ecumenical denominations. They also had a program called Keryx. In that program they dedicated an entire weekend, two times a year, where about 50 volunteers would come in and hold Weekend, and everything revolved around Jesus. *How cool is that?* I was told to get on the waiting list in order to make a Weekend, so I did.

The first couple of years there, everything seemed like heaven. I could go to every Christian service if I wanted to, and I was able to make the first Weekend that they held since I entered the compound. *What a delight!* The men who came in were awesome, so was the food! It didn't matter what religion you were for a Weekend.

I had found that out of the six inmates who were at the table only two or three were believers. In the beginning there was caution, but by the second day all caution was gone and we were forming a family. On the third day many of the men who were not believers accepted Jesus into their hearts.

It was an awesome experience. While there I literally forgot that I was even in prison, *I know what that must sound like, but it is true!* It was a wonderful and Spirit-anointed experience.

Once the Weekend itself was done, the very next week, we had a Keryx meeting. That was where all the candidates and what they called the Inside Team (which was made up of inmates who had already made their own Weekend previously) came together with some of the volunteers. We sang hymns, heard the Word, shared testimonies, and formed small groups to discuss the scriptures. It was great.

In the weeks following less and less of the candidates were showing up. The time came, 6 months later, for the next Keryx Weekend, and I was asked if I would be willing to be part of the Inside Team. Of course, I said yes! It was much more rewarding when I was working, rather than just going through the Weekend. God was doing an awesome work! The Inside Team worked with the Outside Team (the volunteers) to serve in whatever capacity that was needed. The servers served the candidates throughout the Weekend.

In the chapel we prayed for the candidates, the speakers, as well as for each other; and we sang songs glorifying Christ. All the food was prepared in our designated kitchen. Activities and paperwork took place in the Agape room and little sayings of encouragement were placed on individual seats.

Yet, unlike so many wonderful things that God was working through, the follow-up work was really lacking. For a while, after every Weekend the weekly meets were full, but within just a few weeks they dwindled down to only the faithful. Even though Jesus was the center of it all, after some time I found that the work being done was really more emotionally driven then spiritually focused. It confused me as I was witnessing it happen time and time again, and over and over seeing the same results. I experienced a high right after the Weekend, and then a low throughout the 6 month period of time while waiting for the next one.

God was really using me to help the men on the yard, in building them up in their faith, and encouraging them to continue their walk with Christ. One was a man named Jacob, I was his Bunkie at that time, and he and I became very close. We would walk and run together, talking and ministering, just building each other up. He began opening up to me in many areas of his life about the problems he was facing, as well as, some of the fears he had once he was out of prison.

The day came when Jacob received his parole, and was packed up for his transfer to Level 1. We prayed together and before he departed, both of us shed a few tears. Although, he did keep in touch, I would call him and we would write back and forth. I talked to his mom who said everything was going well for him and God was moving within his life. He started up his own lawn care business, he was asked to be a leader in one of the youth groups in his church.

I was pleasantly surprised when one day I received in the mail Jacob's report card. He had told me that he was going back to school for he wanted to become some kind of doctor, the report card had all A's on it. I was so proud of what God was doing within that young man's life. *I know that I had a part of this for coming alongside him.*

God used me to disciple many other brothers; although I only heard from a couple of them after their release date. Others came back because of either transferring from another facility or returned after their release because they fell back into the wages of sin. Through that process, I learned that just because people say they've gotten it doesn't mean they did. So often, what life was for them at one point gets placed on the back burner and they forget to put into practice each and every day what was learned, and the anointing of that word becomes barren in their lives. They become like a dog going back to its own vomit, which is sin.

I also was given a job on the yard crew and placed within the garden area. Back then the yard crew's garden produced all the vegetables that the kitchen used to feed the inmates. To name a few, we grew and harvested tomatoes, onions, cucumbers and radishes. Before long, I was placed in the compost area. It was very hard work, but since I loved the outside and was not afraid of hard work, that was a perfect place for me. It was good for me because in the wintertime, when nobody else was allowed in the garden area, I was the only one out there.

I had to take all the scraps from the kitchen every day and bring them into the compost area. I kept it all shoveled out. It was a very peaceful place to be in the wintertime. Every place I went Christ was with me for it seemed that whatever I put my hands to prospered. Plus, so many people, including some of the officers would come back and ask for prayer for this or that, and that was what I really loved to do. God answered so many of those prayers, a witness to my faith, as well as, the faith of others. Awesome!

One day something happened there that changed everything. The emergency siren went off that morning and we were all told to lock down. An officer had been working in a unit which she usually didn't work in (called non-regulars). She was shaking down a cell and just happened to kick a foot locker of one of the inmates. The whole foot locker fell through the cement floor and disappeared. She had discovered an escape tunnel. The four lifers who had been in the cell had broken through the cement floor and tunneled all the way under the two fences and up next to the road outside of the prison.

The rest of us were locked down for a couple of days over that one. To make matters worse, the facility called in all of the "mob squads" from the other facilities throughout the state. They were made up of officers who were trained to handle riots and extremely dangerous circumstances within prisons.

For the entire night, starting at about 9 p.m. and all the way through until 6 a.m. those mob squads went from unit to unit and floor to floor throughout the facility. They tore up that compound! Not just ripping and raging throughout each cell, but looking for anyone to get smart with them so they could beat them and take them down to the hole. That was a very bad night, to say the least.

The next day the facility walked the warden through the compound for the last time for they forced her into early retirement. It was a sad day all the way around. A new warden was brought in who was nothing but security-minded and the place started to very quickly go downhill.

The following year things really began to change. Gang members started to pour in and the warden refused to allow any of his "good guys" to transfer out which, literally, created a bad environment. By not being allowed to transfer out, people who were there just laying back and doing their time began to feel like they were being punished for doing good. The facility became more and more violent.

Stabbings were becoming an everyday occurrence. Things started to go from bad to worse. Many homosexuals were being brought in and sexual activities were happening everywhere. They even started to create a business out of it using one of the programs as a front. People would get placed on the call out for that program just to have sexual favors performed for a fee. Then, if that wasn't bad enough, the state decided to remove cigarettes from all facilities. For many, cigarettes had become a business.

Once tobacco became illegal, the prices went up for purchasing whatever tobacco was left on the compound, and for those who still owed money, if they couldn't pay right then, they got butchered. Within a three week period, there were at least 300 stabbings and many fights. That, in turn, created an even more violent atmosphere. Before I left, around three ambulances came in every single day for someone that had been stuck or beaten with a lock, or had been gang raped.

During that time, I was very close to a brother who was one of the main leaders within the church. He was the chaplain's clerk and in charge of the chaplain's library. I was with him almost every day. That brother had been locked up for more than 30 years and had a very violent past. Before I really started to know him he had a very hard exterior, never smiled, and was always serious. I remember times when I would walk into the library and just be hit by a wall of anger, yet some days the room was filled with peace.

I noticed that the more I remained in my joyful, Spirit-filled self that the anointing would powerfully rest upon that brother, and I began to see a wonderful change within him. To everyone, he was happier and more joyful to be around. Through him, God began to powerfully open doors for me. I was made to be one of the leaders of the Keryx program, both within the Weekend itself and the weekly meetings.

During that time, the Assembly of God church service that was held there, started to turn in a different direction. The pastors were a husband and wife team who began to drastically change. The wife started preaching every message. *I think the Jezebel spirit came upon her, maybe it was always there?* She began wearing tight, revealing clothing, and completely took over the church services. Prior to that, the worship there was awesome, but every time that woman stepped up to preach I just cringed. Something was very wrong!

God told me that I had to speak to both of them, and to say that she was being led astray and needed to repent; otherwise God was going to remove them from the church. I prayed about it, then asked them both to speak with me in the hallway. I told them what God had said. The woman threw her hands up in the air and told me that I was not from God, and stormed back into the service. The following week God told me to repeat the same words to them, and I did. Again, she threw up her hands and said, "Oh, this again!" She stormed back into the service.

I didn't go back to that service again, but switched to the Baptist service. From that moment on, many people started to tell me that I was a prophet. Like all the other times before, I would tell them, "No, I'm not". However, there was one Spirit-filled brother, always with a smile on his face and a good word to give, who would call me nothing but, "Prophet Anthony". Regardless of how much I persisted for him not to call me that, it was the only way he would address me.

Years later at another facility, a brother who had also been with me at the Dark Place, told me that he always used me as part of his testimony. I didn't understand and so I asked him what he meant by that. He revealed to me that after I rebuked the Assembly of God pastors, that the woman had come back into the service and very sarcastically said, "Anthony just told me that I am not of God and that God will close this service if I don't repent." He said she often laughed about that and every chance she got, mocked me. The brother went on to say that within a year that couple was asked to leave and to not come back. In fact, that denomination was completely removed from the facility. The brother went on to say, it was for that reason he used me as a source of how God still speaks through people, and that there are still prophets today in the midst of the church. *God is amazing!*

There was a problem within the church and it was weighing heavy on my mind. Many, including the leaders, feared the chaplain's clerk because of his temper. Rather than confronting him directly, they continually came to me because I was friends with the man. I began to see a trend happening, people found it easier to pawn off their responsibilities upon others when they didn't want to deal with things themselves, the chaplain's clerk being one of those "things"! I found myself having a heart toward the man, yet frustrated at everyone else for their lack of confidence.

One day as I was walking the yard I looked up and saw a very precious sight, it was Brother Alex. He was the one who, at a previous facility, was instrumental in helping me create a worship service during a time when there was no chaplain on board. Brother Alex had been delivered from a life of homosexuality and he so loved the Lord. It was so nice to be around him, definitely a bright light in a very dark place. So, of course, he and I were always together building, praying and sharing the Word with everyone.

I felt certain God had given Brother Alex, the chaplain's clerk and myself, that compound to use for His glory, and I was looking forward to seeing how powerful God would move through the three of us. But, the chaplain's clerk began to drastically change.

The chaplain's clerk began to change right before my eyes, his entire attitude went from friend to foe. Once again, that same presence of anger had begun manifesting itself whenever one would enter his library. It seemed as though jealousy overtook his heart and he had become bitter and angry. At every turn, a spirit of hatefulness and strife flooded every Christian activity which was happening on the compound. Because of him, the Keryx program had begun to crumble from the inside out.

Because of the division that had been created between Brother Alex and the chaplain's clerk, it was as if a spirit of anger was within the church. Other brothers, who were at one time on fire for the Lord, started to turn from their faith; many tried to commit suicide. I, too, felt weaker.

One day, while I was working in the gardens, I was listening to a radio station, called, 'Smile FM'. One of the women announcers who came on the air had just returned from a 6-month maternity leave after delivering twin girls. The other announcer asked a question which was for me a life changing teaching from the Lord.

As she was speaking to the other announcer she said, "I always wondered why God made babies to crawl and move around before He made them to speak. It would be so much easier if they could just tell me what they needed rather than crying until I figure out what it is that they want. I may never know until I get to heaven and be able to ask God why."

I questioned the same thing when I thought back to the truth of that question. God spoke to me and said so clearly, "As I created children to first walk and then speak, so have I created my children to first walk in the Spirit in order for them to be able to speak in my anointing." He went on to say, "If my people cannot walk by faith in their lives, then they cannot speak under Divine Inspiration."

I began feasting on that thought which God had so wonderfully planted within me. I began to seek this thing out through the scriptures and oh how God so mightily revealed His righteousness. This is the revelation of His righteousness granted to us.

This revelation of His righteousness really helped me

out during this time of weakness within my soul. It had such an impact within me that I started to preach it to everyone and everywhere! While running, while in the chaplain's library, in the garden, and to whomever I was walking with. But the people just were not getting it like I did. They loved their complacency and did not want to come out of their sins. They were satisfied with Jesus only being their Savior, but to be sold out and making Jesus their Lord was not on their agenda. Once again, the weakness and sorrow came flooding back into my soul. I felt trapped! No matter how much I prayed or fasted, I could not seem to shake the darkness that was around me.

During that time, I had a roommate who was getting approximately ten letters every day. Always having a longing for God to bring a wife into my life, I asked him how he was getting so many letters. He gave me an application to "Write a Prisoner.com". I longed for some type of companionship from a woman, so I created a profile and sent it to them along with my picture, and the fee that they charged. Within a few weeks I received a letter from a woman who was up north near one of the facilities where I was formerly housed.

Within two or three weeks, the word marriage came up. *Well, I have to go now!* I stopped writing her. Then I received a letter which started out, "You do not know me, but I am writing in regards to get the nagging image of your face out of my mind." *What?* I really couldn't do anything but laugh. She was a blessing in many ways, yet in others, because of my spiritual condition of weakness and loneliness, our relationship started to go in the wrong direction. We started to write sex letters to each other. Things from there could really go no other place but down. Yet, God, somehow kept us together as friends.

Before being incarcerated, I had been in a relationship with a woman named Sarah. She was amazing in every way. Even though I had no idea what love was, I was in love with her! I took her for granted as so many men do and seeing how the only way I knew how to love was through sex, we forged our relationship around that. I did very much love her. We were even engaged for a short period of time. When I committed the crime which brought me to prison, Sarah and I were not together, even though we were sleeping together.

When I first met Sarah she was pure in almost every way and by the time that I was arrested she had such a cold and hardened heart and it was all because of me. I longed for God to bring a wife into my life who I could pour my love into, which I was never able to give to her.

So, when I met Karen through Write a Prisoner.com, I clung to her in hopes that she could be my wife. She did help me through a lot while I was at the dark place. For the very short period of time we knew each other, we definitely had our ups and downs, but she was a friend, *and I praise God for her even to this present day.*

Around that same time period, Alex and I started a fast for revival within the compound. We set out to do a forty day fast, eating only one meal a day. I was so desperate to see God move within the hearts of the men there. However, I was even more desperate to see revival within my own life.

I started to fast, no meals a day for a seven day period. But then things just seemed to get worse for me. I went back to eating one meal a day, and within a week or two I ate nothing for another seven days. By the time we finished the forty day fast I felt as though I was in a worse condition than before! All I saw was anger rising up within me.

During the fast, one night I was on my bunk and on my knees praying when God brought me into a vision.

I was looking over the three garden fields that were situated on the compound. They were bare, as if it was March or April. The land, too, was bare, but the soil was prepared. It started to rain and I saw things beginning to grow within the gardens, but as I looked closer I saw only weeds. It continued to rain and the weeds grew thicker until the gardens were so full nothing else could have grown there.

I came out of the vision and found myself on the bunk still on my knees. The vision had seemed so real and I was more confused than ever. I prayed, "God, what does this mean?" I heard His ever still small voice come up from my spirit saying to me, "The gardens are the people on the compound. The rain that came down was your prayers." Immediately, I interrupted, "Then why were weeds the only things growing? That is all I see here within the people's hearts and I don't understand*!" I so love the patience of God, for He just continued as if I never broke in on what He was saying.* "The reason why the weeds grew and overtook all the gardens is because that is what happens when all you do is

70

pray, but never plant any seeds. Prayers are worthless if there are no seeds to be watered." Wow! I just didn't know how to handle that. I really wanted to scream at God, but knowing that if I did it would have come out as an actual scream and I would have woke my three roommates. In frustration and weakness, I began to cry. I thought I had planted seeds within the people's hearts. How could God tell me that I didn't plant seeds? For the rest of the night, I felt defeated and could only cry out to God.

After that I began to wake up every morning with anger in my heart. I also found that I was losing my love for God's people. I still feasted on God's Word as much as I could, and prayed during the night hours. I began to draw back from the church and just draw closer to Jesus. Due to my broken soul, there were so many times where nothing seemed to matter, I found no relief. To make matters worse for me, the church services started to increase, but not as I had hoped.

I began to see men holding hands and sitting really close to each other. People who I knew had no heart for God were showing up, and the services started to become as dark as my soul felt.

I can't explain it, but I felt empty and alone, even though I was a leader of the church and of the services. There were four elders who took rotation on coordinating and giving a word at the beginning of each service. Every four weeks, I was up to coordinate and to give a word before we entered into worship.

I began to seek out why all of these people, who I knew

did not want to change, were coming into the only place where I found any type of peace. *The Word tells us that if we seek we will find. Well, I found another battle.* There were a few people who were going around and pawning off their responsibilities upon the church services. *What I mean by that is, God has given each of us the word of reconciliation, and we are to lead people to the Lord Jesus Christ, then welcome them to come to church as born again believers. This is called discipleship!* I tried explaining to those few guys that to invite sin-ruled people to church who are not focused on evangelism was not wise, because the volunteers (preachers or teachers) come with the intent to encourage and strengthen the body of Christ. Sin really is not even declared to be an enemy, or that the only way to escape sin is through Jesus Christ. So, those men, who were sin-ruled were coming in and were being strengthened in their sins, rather than being convicted to deny their sins. They became worse than when they first started coming to the services. They were leaving encouraged in the condition which they were in, all the while sin was abounding even more within their lives. Again, I found that people just wanted to pawn off their spiritual responsibilities unto others. *I guess it is easier to just invite unconverted souls to church thinking that they will hear the Word there, which would be true if the services were geared for that, but because they were not, they were devastating the church community.*

The more I told the men to preach the Word, asking the people to make a commitment to make Jesus Lord and Savior of their lives, the more they did the opposite. More and more, active homosexuals were coming in. *When I think about it, of course, they were coming in...because it was the one place they were not convicted about the truth of their lifestyle, which kept them from God, rather than being drawn closer to Him!*

I grew angrier for two reasons. First, they were taking the only place where I found rest for my soul. Secondly, they were twisting the truth and becoming bolder in their sins. I longed to be bolder in His holiness, righteousness and power. Yet, there were those people who loved to sin, doing the unthinkable and with it finding peace. Ultimately, even though, back then, I couldn't see it, *I do now, for I think that all of this was happening to make me face something that I hated within my own life.*

When I was eight years old, I was not raped, but I was molested by a man whom I did not know. What the man did to me, and then forced me to do to him, didn't hurt, but I felt really dirty and I knew afterward that it was wrong. To make matters worse, a few years later I was placed in another circumstance when the same thing happened. Being that I was so young at the time, I did not know anything about homosexuals. Later I learned of homosexuals, and I immediately blamed them for creating within me a dirty desire in which I masked with hatred. *Now, these people were taking over the Lord's church services.* I prayed and prayed against what was happening.

The day came for me to once again coordinate the church service. That morning I heard the Lord tell me to "throw the spear". I immediately knew what spear He was talking about. The scripture came to mind of Phinehas. "And when Phinehas…saw it, he rose up from among the congregation, and took a javelin in his hand; and he went after the man of Israel into the tent, and thrust both of them through, the man of Israel, and the woman through her belly. So the plague was stayed from the children of Israel." (Numbers 25:7-8) I prayed for courage to come into my soul. The moment came for me to give a ten minute word to the people and I threw the spear.

I started by saying that I was not addressing this to anyone who had come out of homosexuality. Rather, to the people who were participating in homosexual acts within the services (yes, they were committing homosexual acts during the church services!) I then received such an anointed boldness, and I told every one of them to get out! I told them that they were not welcome in God's house!

Then I went to another deadly plague that was being spread by certain men who came in. Those men were adamant that Jesus was not God, but only a prophet and a man. I told them to get out! After that, everyone in the entire place was in shock. I, too, was a bit shocked and I knew what was coming!

After the service, the elders and a bunch of people within the church tore into me, up one side and down the other. They said that they wanted all the homosexuals and the other men there, and that they were not going to leave. They threatened me and said I was the one who was going to leave. I shared with one of the elders who was angry and furious toward me, that Jesus "…did not come to bring peace, but a sword". (Matthew 10:34) He began yelling, stating that Jesus did not say that, and that He only came to bring peace.

Again, I found myself crying out to God, knowing He had told me to throw the spear. From that moment I tried everything on the church, even stated that they could excommunicate me from all services. They did not succeed which made them even more furious toward me.

I would be walking and people would get right in my face and threaten me, in fact, I was threatened quite a few times. As I walked the black top during night yard, I was always bumping into people. (The black top is a stretch of black pavement about 500 feet long and 150 feet wide with an average of about 1500 people on it every night.) Of course, there were stabbings out there every single night. Many never got caught, others so bloody that they could not hide from anyone, let alone the officers.

On those nights as I walked the length of the black top I would pray and seek God. The atmosphere was thick with an evil presence. Regardless of how blind one was to spiritual things, it was very noticeable that the atmosphere had a dark, thickness to it. God stood with me fulfilling the promise of His Word which was, "The Lord is with me as a dread warrior; therefore my persecutors will stumble; they will not overcome me." (Jeremiah 20:11) Not one of their threats were brought to fruition, not one of them!

At that time, I was working as a barber. One day as I

was cutting hair I saw a Deputy Warden talking to one of the officers. She knew of me by all the Keryx Weekends that I was involved in and knew that I always helped the chaplain. I had just previously put in a kite requesting to be transferred. I knew it was a long shot, seeing how the Warden was not letting any of his "good guys" transfer out. As I was looking at her, the Spirit of God just so softly told me to go over by her, so I did. As soon as she saw me, I, literally, saw God open her eyes toward me. She said to me, "Isn't your name, Anthony?" I told her it was and I asked how she was doing. She told me, "Just fine, thanks for asking." One week later I was told to pack up for I was being transferred out! *Oh hallelujah to Jesus!!!*

The following morning I was sent to the visiting room to wait until time for me to leave. When I got there, I saw about 40 people who were excited about leaving. It took about an hour and a half for them to process us and get us on the Snow Bird (which was what we called the transfer bus.) No sooner than we got off the grounds, an assurance and a peace washed over me. We got about an hour or so into the long trip down state when over the radio we heard a guy shouting on the air that he was outside the correctional facility (*the one I had just left*) where there had been an attempted escape. Then the guy started shouting, "Oh, my God! They just shot him! They shot him!"

A part of me wanted to listen intently, while the other part of me was so glad to be out of there. All of a sudden the Spirit of God spoke to me and said, "I know how to deliver the righteous out of the hands of the wicked." Immediately, a peace washed over me again, I felt like crying. I later found out that four lifers stole a truck, which was on the compound, and had driven it through all three fences.

One of the escapees was a man named Maxwell, who jumped out of the truck and ran toward freedom. A prison officer who was driving around the perimeter shot Maxwell in the head, killing him.

Several times in the past, I had tried ministering to Maxwell, but he could not believe that God would forgive him. He had killed seven of his own family members. I wasn't sure if God was willing to forgive and love a man like myself, so I can only imagine what Maxwell thought. I can understand why he didn't accept Jesus, but that hadn't stopped me from offering the priceless, free gift to him.

7

ANOTHER TRANSFER

We drove to the next correctional facility and viewed the sign bearing its name. I started to pray, for the only thing I had heard of that prison was the name the officers had given it, Bloody Creek.

I was given the unit and cell numbers and I found that it was the Re-entry Program unit. Half of the unit consisted of people who were going home within a maximum of 60 days.

Like every other prison that I had been in, I spent the first two weeks just sitting back and observing what was happening on the compound. *Who are Christians, and who are not, and who are the people they are hanging out with?* Throughout the years I had found that just by watching everyday activities, was a huge part of not getting caught up with the wrong people, no matter what they claimed to be.

The place was run like a Level 4, even though there were only two units for Level 4 and three units for Level 2. It was completely different from the dark place where there had been no order. There were big yellow lines going down all the walk ways which we were not allowed to cross over. If we left our cells we had to have our shirts tucked in, unless we were on the big yard. *Even though when I was on the outside I had hated rules and wouldn't abide by them, now I'm finding comfort in all of these rules... Amazing!* I received a part time job on the yard crew.

The church services were pretty weak in the anointing, but I was away from all the unholy things that destroyed that at the last facility. It was nice just to be able to go to a service and have no part of leadership or have people coming to ask me for this or that. I could just be there. All the songs we sang were from Keryx books, which was good because I knew all the words.

Another church service they held there was similar to a bible study. Volunteers came in, we would sing a couple of songs, have a small word and break off into groups, like the Keryx weekly meetings. I was able for the first time to share and speak of some of the hardships and hurts which were deeply engraved within my soul. With individual believers, I shared my faith and the revelations which God had given to me.

For the first time since being incarcerated, I did not want to get to know the facility's worship leader. I wanted no part of leadership at all! For the first few months, I stayed away from the leader.

Except for my cell mates, I walked and spent time with only one brother, whose name was Mason. He was a young man who was always hungry to hear the Word. We had great discussions about our faith. God used him so mightily to help me heal. Just him being there, walking, talking, needing nothing but friendship, but he wanted to hear the Word of God. *I praise God for that brother!*

When at the dark place, I had been introduced to a worship leader (in the world) named, Kari Jobe, and I had fallen in love with her anointing. At my new surroundings, I shared one of her songs with Brother Mason. I don't even remember which song it was, but I gave him the MP3 player and within a minute he handed the player back to me and said, "Dude, I am not going to be crying on the yard!" I couldn't help but laugh. Her voice was so powerful and moving,

One day I was working out in the weight pit with Mason. Because he was coming down with a cold, I was ministering the Word of God to him concerning healing. A black guy came over to us and said that he believed in miracles and healing. The guy shared a testimonial of his encounter with God's power while he was in my hometown county jail.

He said, "There was a minister who would come in every month or so to preach. That minister once gave an altar call to accept Christ into your heart, and/or to receive healing. I went up to the altar because my left leg was shorter than my right leg by about two inches, and my back was messed up due to a football injury."

The man went on to say, "I tell you the truth…that minister laid his hands on me and my leg, literally, grew out; and my back was instantly healed! I've never had a problem with either of them since that night." He continued, "I believe in miracles."

I said, "That is wonderful!" Then I asked him who the minister was, and when I heard the name I stood in awe! He said, "The man's name is Pastor Van. I have his address; do you want it?"

"Do I want it? Yeah, I want it!" When I was about ten years old, it was that minister who gave me my first encounter with God. He laid hands on me and I went down. *"Oh God, You are awesome!"* After that, I tried to get in contact with Pastor Van via letter, but to date, haven't heard from him.

After about 6 months of being there, I started fellowshipping with a few men who were using their yard time to practice the songs they were going to do in church the following Sunday. I joined them to sing to Jesus, and for some quality time with the brothers.

A week later, the worship leader packed up and went home. That left a vacancy. Nobody wanted to step up and lead the singing. Nobody! I encouraged the brothers to fill the position, even saying I would help, but they tried to make me the worship leader. I said, "Oh, no! I want nothing to do with leading anything!" I refused to lead.

When Sunday came they really stumbled in leading worship. Afterward, I again joined them on the yard and tried to help them. We sounded great on the yard; however, when the following Sunday came again they stumbled over the singing. Still nobody would step up in leading them.

"Fine! I will lead the worship!" Then I told God, "I don't see why you are calling me to do this when I can't even keep a beat; I can't even clap with everyone else."

For the next month, every time we began a song I would encourage the people and get them lifted up in spirit, and the worship was anointed. For the first time since being there, everyone was on their feet singing and clapping, lifting their hands and setting their faces toward heaven. It was really amazing! I still fought every step of the way though, for I did not want to lead anything!

After about six months of being there, I was called to the classification office and offered the barber job. I was happy to get off the yard crew for I was only getting about 8 dollars a month. Since the barber job was a skilled one I would get a higher wage, although I knew I would not be getting much pay the first month.

While cutting hair I was able to minister to so many people, including many of the officers. I remember one night after work, I was cleaning up and an officer came into the barber shop and handed me a pack of tuna fish. He said that he had taken it from someone who brought it into the school, and we were not allowed to bring anything into the school building. God had given me so much favor that this officer gave it to me, rather than throwing it away like he was supposed to do. *God, you are awesome!*

The time came when I was to receive a full month's pay, but I was disappointed. I looked at the statement before me and I had received 10 dollars for the entire month. *What? This has got to be wrong!* I checked into it for I was supposed to be making around 35-40 dollars a month with that job. I discovered that they were only giving me half my wages in order to 'save money'. I was really upset!

I wrote a kite to the deputy warden who was over all

jobs on the compound, telling him that I had only received 10 dollars for the entire month. I told him that it was theft and misappropriation of funds. I received the kite back saying that if I fail to work an entire eight hours that they can pay me for a half day's work. Then, within a week, I was called back to the unit from the barber shop. I stepped into the unit as the officer was coming down the stairs. He noticed me and began to wave his fingers at me as if to say, 'bye'. I was transferring out! *Oh hallelujah to Jesus!*

Before time to go, I went and talked to a couple of the fellas who were in the worship team. The one who was leading at the time started to panic. "We can't lose you!" With tears in his eyes and shaking his head, he said, "We need you here, I can't do what you do. I am not ready for this."

I told him that God believed that he was ready and that God would not disappoint him, everything would be alright. I almost cried for I had wanted nothing to do with leading anything, yet God had used me in such a powerful way. That brother was in tears because I was leaving, and others expressed sadness when I talked to them.

Having bought a TV from 'off the streets' (that is what it's called when it has been purchased from another person). I knew that I could not take it with me because it wasn't bought legally. I planned to give it to Mason once I was actually ready to depart, for he didn't have one. *I can't help but laugh...*the officer who packed me up in the day room was known for being a hard officer. So when another brother came into the room and in front of the officer asked if I wanted him to grab my TV for me, I had to say that I didn't have one, even though there was one sitting on the stand in my cell. The officer looked up at the guy who had offered to help and said, "Don't front Anthony off!" The officer then looked at me and smiled. *What favor!* That officer had every right to go down to my cell and take the TV right then and there. Every hard thing that people had said about that officer may have been true, yet he showed me favor and smiled while doing it. *Awesome!* The next day, I was told to go up front and I was able to hand off the TV to Mason, give him a hug and tell him, "God bless you!" *I so love my God!*

During the eight months when I was on that compound, God so wonderfully used that facility as a healing place for me. As others complained about how bad things were, I just drew closer to God. Very slowly, I had, once again, found that my love was growing for God's people.

8

HE HAS BROUGHT ME
BACK FULL CIRCLE

They put us on the bus and off we went. As we were riding down the road, I was looking at all the beautiful scenery and I began to think about what God had told me before I left Level 4; that I would be going to the three worst prisons in the state. I was then leaving the third worst prison that God had told me I was to go.

While riding, I reminisced…I was at my first transfer for about eight months, and a few years later I heard that facility had been condemned and closed. God brought into my remembrance how I had kicked the dust off my feet before leaving there, then he closed it down. Wow! *Praise God!* I was at the dark place for 5 years to the day. *Now, I'm leaving yet another facility.* I believe the location of my first transfer was the worst in being spiritually dead. The dark place, deemed as the most assaultive facility in the state 3years in a row, while I was there. The third year was worse than both of the previous two years. Then there was my other transfer which was also an assaultive facility before I left Level 4; it changed to a very dry, legalistic and a fearful place. When a fight broke out in Level 4, the officers would shut the entire facility down and we would be locked in our cells until the next day. Nobody, not even the chaplain, could really get any movement of the Spirit going, the facility would always stop it. Whenever the name of that facility came up, there wasn't anything good spoken about it; but for me, *praise God,* it was a much needed healing place.

After a couple of hours on the road we pulled up to a prison and I observed the big sign in front which read: "Level 4 Correctional Facility". Hallelujah to Jesus! *He has brought me back full circle.*

I received my unit and cell number and to my surprise, I was put in the same unit which I had previously left. I entered the unit and was recognized by a very dear brother named Ruben. What a smile and embrace I received from him.

Revival was all that was on Ruben's mind. When he saw me, he said, "God is going to move now that you're back!" I just laughed, even though within, I was still so very broken.

For the first two weeks I became reacquainted with many of the brothers whom I had known from when I was there the first time. It was awesome! It wasn't long before I was called out to pick up my hobby craft. When I came out of the hobby craft room I ran into a very beloved man, my old Food Tech teacher, The Boss.

I wasn't sure if The Boss would even remember me; but before I could even ask, with a huge smile on his face, he reached out and shook my hand. As we walked to the Food Tech room, he turned to face me once again telling me that if I was interested to send a kite and he would get me back into class. *What?* "Yes! Yes, I will!" I was so excited. *I love cooking and there isn't anyone I'd rather look up to than The Boss.* I couldn't help but think, "Why me, God?" *Favor after favor God has poured out to me.* I certainly did not feel as though I deserved it, but God was showing me that it is in our brokenness, that he revives.

I also saw a brother with whom I had spent so much time with while I was there before, whose name was Isaac. I expected to witness the same person who I knew before I left. He had been on fire for God and was so wonderfully full of the Holy Spirit. *Now all I see and hear from Isaac is a shadow of the man I used to know.* His entire demeanor was different. He was talking about Jesus, but not like before. He then stated he wasn't sure if he had ever been saved in the first place.

My spirit broke for Isaac and I could not understand what had happened. I tried speaking to him a few more times but when we talked he had kept his distance from me. I had heard from Alex, (who spent time at Level 4 before being moved to the dark place) that he had known Isaac and another brother who were both walking powerfully in the Spirit.

However, the more that Alex told me about the other guy, the more that my spirit sent up red flags. In presenting the Word to Alex, he too, began seeing the error of the other brother's teachings. I began connecting the dots with Isaac and I asked him about the other brother. He started telling me about all the great things that the guy had done, but all the "works" that both Alex and Isaac were telling me were all done many years ago at another facility. I found out that the other guy was a false prophet and was living purely on an old experience, *not on fresh revelations of the here and now*. Every time I had a room opening I asked Isaac if he wanted to move in with me, for he was in the same cell with the false prophet. Every time Isaac said, "No".

The leaders of the church services asked me if I wanted to be a part of the leadership board. I thought that I might be ready so I said, "Yes", but within a few months I had to step down. I found myself getting into another battle with depression. Each week when I had to get up and deliver a word of encouragement to the people, it was just too stressful. Anxiety would just overtake me. Each time I was to coordinate the service, I would lose all focus and desire to preach or to encourage anyone, or, for that matter, to do anything.

I told the brothers who were looked to as leaders there that I was not ready, and I entered further into a season of depression. I fell back into the old addiction of watching TV all day long and not wanting to minister or pray over people. Once again, I was falling back into a lack of love toward the body.

Deeper and deeper I went into that depression, it was overwhelming. I didn't know how to get out of it, all I saw spiritually was darkness. Everywhere I looked, I was seeing evil, so much evil. The facility was nothing like The Dark Place, yet I could not help but look at everything through the eyes that I had when I was there. Though difficult to explain, all I could see was the bad, and it was bringing me into a darker place of depression.

One day as I was reading the Word and praying for God to deliver me from the darkness, He brought me into remembrance of a revelation which he had previously given to me. It was about sowing and reaping. Again, He revealed that if I wanted to experience His love, then I would have to put my feelings aside, and by faith, sow acts of love.

I needed to sow acts of love, for the more I sowed, greater would be the harvest. Same thing with joy, or peace, or anything dealing with God's promises to us. Faith calls those things that are not, as if they were already done. *This is how faith operates*. In order to fully walk in love, I needed the joy of the Lord to be my strength. Jesus gave me a revelation of a scripture which changed my view of getting the victory back into my life. "I had fainted, unless I had believed to see the goodness of the Lord in the land of the living." (Psalm 27:13) I could not see His goodness in the people or place I was, because I was too focused on all the hurt and pain of where I used to be.

The spirit brought me into remembrance of another verse, "Truly, if they had been mindful of that country from whence they came out, they might have had an opportunity to have returned." (Hebrews 11:15) I was so mindful on what used to be, rather than on what was. Standing on the Word, unless I believed to see the goodness of the Lord in the land of the living, I would faint.

I began to put it into practice. It was not easy at all in the beginning, for some days the only thing that I would see was someone opening a door for someone else. If that was all that I saw, then that would be enough. I would focus on that one good deed and I began to rejoice and give God praise, both within my spirit and verbally, seeing the goodness of the Lord in the land of the living.

While doing that, the Lord told me, "It is impossible for you to love me, if you can't love the church, for we are one and the same." *That blew me away! What a needed revelation!* From that day on, as I loved and looked to Jesus I was somehow able to look at the body of Christ, no longer seeing them as the dark place. I started to wake up believing that I would see the goodness of the Lord in that facility, and within His people. Even before I ever physically saw anything, I began to rejoice. The joy of the Lord was flooding back into my soul.

Once the joy and love of God started to come back into my life, there was one place in my heart where I felt the tugging of God. *If there is one thing that I know about God, it is, He will never touch anything that we are not willing to face or give to Him. He is a perfect gentleman.* Because I hadn't felt worthy enough to face it, the insecurity which I had fled from time and time again, grew within my heart. Honestly, I thought that if I did face it and make it known, I'd be hurt again.

From the beginning I fell hard in love with Jesus. In time, I fell in love with the Holy Spirit. I would always come to them. I would pray using the word, "Father", but

I would never pray to the Father. For twelve years I never once addressed or came to God the Father in prayer, for the simple reason: *I had no idea of how to be a son.*

I was a horrible son to my mom, and I had no father figure in my life. I so longed to have a relationship with God, that I could see Him as my father; but also, I longed to be a better son than before to my mom. When I was out in the streets, I didn't even consider my mom to be family. *Now, here she is, my best friend, being the mother that I never allowed her to be prior to my being incarcerated.*

I so wanted to give my mom that gift which I did not yet possess. I didn't see or feel worthy enough to be a son, especially a son of God; although God was bringing me into a situation where I could face it. I started to pray about those things. I wanted to break free from the insecurity within my life and come boldly unto the Father as the Word of God promises me I can do.

It took several days of praying and exploring the unchartered territories of my heart for Jesus to come in. I was standing on the promise, "If a man loves me, he will keep my Words: and My Father will love him, and we will come unto him, and make our dwelling with him." (John 14:23)

I believe it was on the third day of seeking God, I had been in prayer for about an hour or two, when God brought me into a vision.

I was in His throne room, and I saw Jesus. As if I was

just a little child, He came and picked me up in His arms and held me tight for a moment; then placed me into the lap of the Father. I could not see His face for the brightness was too much, but the love that streamed from Him was amazing! I curled up in the Father's lap, never having felt safer in my life. He didn't say one word to me, rather just held me in His loving arms. It felt like I was there just a few minutes when I found myself on my knees and on my bunk, crying. No longer because of an unworthy feeling or doubt, for I had a new assurance. I was fully accepted as a son in the heart of the Father. He had come and made His dwelling within me.

I looked at my watch and realized that what had seemed to be just a few minutes with the Father had actually been an hour that had passed. *God is so good to me. I now continually say, "I am a perfectly spoiled child." And I love it!*

Around that time, God brought a guy named Justin onto the compound, and what an anointing that man had. He, being a prophet, confirmed by the things he was able to see and call forth within from people, was his gift. Almost immediately, I fell under his discipleship. I saw many people set free from their past. There were not many physical healings or miracles, but it was amazing the way in which Justin was able to see things and how much he knew.

Justin was there about 8 months to a year before he was released. Before he left, I, too, received so many of the same revelations he had gotten from the Word. Walking the yard together, I remember thinking to myself, "Finally a brother who can actually encourage and keep up with me in the Word of God!" He would continuously tell me that I was called into the office of the prophet. He would say that he recognized in me the same spirit and anointing that was upon him.

Although I did not openly reject this word like I had done so many times before when others called me a prophet, I still had a wall within my soul toward it. Justin continually made promises that he would keep in contact with me once he was out. That really blessed my soul, especially since there were many who made that promise. However, only two people in my past who were from the Dark Place had actually kept their word, Abe and Jacob. Abe had stopped writing after a few months of getting in contact with me and Jacob died.

The day came when Justin was to go home. He was 60 years old and leaving with nothing. We were able to have regular street clothes for visits back then, so I gave him my best visiting outfit, a brand new pair of socks, and my favorite T-shirt. (On that shirt I had a guy paint a picture with the hands of Jesus holding a skull dripping with blood. Two golden skeleton keys were behind the hands. In back of the keys was a chess board with black pieces on one side and white pieces on the other which represented our decisions in life. There were golden skyscrapers with rays of light shining from them behind the chess board which represented the city of God in heaven. *It kind of breaks my heart because since Justin left I have yet to hear from him.*

A few months after Justin went home I had the privilege

of moving in with a dear brother by the name of Nate. We had bible studies daily and each night we would have a time of prayer together. Wow, what a time that was! Nate grew so much spiritually. He switched to the same bible that I used, which was The Hebrew Greek Key Word Study Bible, but instead of the King James Version (KJV) he got the New King James Version (NKJV). He loved it!

There were times when we were in prayer and the presence of God so powerfully showed up that it became tangible to the both of us. The first few times Nate came out of our prayer baffled and in awe of what he had just experienced, and saying, "I have never experienced God like that before!"

Within a few months Nate was told to pack up, he was being transferred to the Level 1 facility next door. Because he was only given a half hour to pack we did not have much time at all to grieve with each other over his departure. However, I did take the opportunity to ask Isaac (the one who was under really bad teaching) if he wanted to move in with me. Again, he declined my invitation.

I was called to the desk and told that I needed to go to the Food Tech classroom. I actually said to the officer, "Oh, yah!" I knew that if I was being called to see The Boss it meant that I was getting into his class. Sure enough, I walked over there and he had, once again, made a way for me to get into the class. Even though I had taken the class when I was first at Level 4, I never finished because I needed the money. We were not allowed to go to school and have a job at the same time.

Technically, the "Lifers" were not able to take job training classes because they had no out date. The school only went by a list of earliest release dates of the prisoners, Once again I stood before the much cherished man, and The Boss extended a hand of favor toward me.

The following week I, once again, started in the Food Tech 1-year program. The one thing I was most excited about was that Brother Isaac was the clerk. Throughout my time as a student, daily I was able to minister, talk with, and encourage him. A few times while in the class that I had an empty room and I asked Isaac if he wanted to get moved in, but he still said, "No."

When time came for me to graduate, I was trying to stick around as long as I could without The Boss telling me that I had to get out of the class. One day as I came in, I heard that the only tutor was packing up and transferring to Level 1. The Boss offered me the job, and of course I took it, and almost gave him a huge hug! Not only was I a tutor, doing what I loved to do, cooking food, but I was also working with a very dear brother. It really touched my heart. *How awesome is God?!*

Having an active, solid Christian chaplain was a real blessing to us, but with doing the work of both chaplaincy and all the hobby craft duties, the man was just too overworked. The facility forced the original chaplain over to the Level 1 facility, and in time hired a woman from off the streets to be the full time chaplain. It was an extraordinary thing that she had such a heart for the men who resided there.

That woman chaplain went through so much garbage from the administration that she would say, "It took me coming to prison to be introduced to the devil." She was confronted with spiritual warfare for the first time in her life. The administration hated the fact that she cared so much for the prisoners. The officers would treat her worse than they treated us.

The female chaplain was really big into music so she focused a lot of her time in furnishing the worship team with new equipment. She was able to purchase regular and electric guitars, an electric drum set, microphones, a keyboard, and other things, too numerous to count. There was no way she was supposed to be able to get any of that, but by the favor of God she somehow managed it. Such a blessing she was to all of us. Due to the administration there, she had to call it quits and retired after she made it two full years.

After that blessed sister retired, the facility hired a chaplain who was already working in that capacity for the Department of Corrections. That chaplain was a black man in his late fifties who came in with an iron fist. He broke all the traditions that we had and he turned things upside down. I loved it!

Even though at times it may not be wanted, I love change! When things change we break free from all our old traditions and the Lord can just have His way with and through us. I have always found that the Spirit's work blossoms so much more when things are in a changing position.

The first week there another chaplain removed everyone who was in a leadership position, except the one who was coordinating for that week, a brother who was an older black man and very set in his ways. That brother chose to use his last name rather than his first and it actually fit him perfectly. Literally, his last name was, 'Pride'.

In time, the chaplain's true passion started to be revealed which was, 'Lifers'. That was cool! One Saturday, before the church service began, he pulled me to the side and asked if I would give a 3-minute testimony. I was glad to be asked to do so, for I believe if you are walking by faith, then you will always be able to share a good report.

I gave my testimony. I believe it was from that moment on, coupled with my constant joy and passion for the people, that the chaplain started to single me out by telling everyone that I was the example for the church to follow.

I remember during one service, the people in the front were filled with excitement, but the ones toward the back barely clapped their hands or sang with any passion. In order to motivate them I decided to sit in the back. The chaplain began the service, then stopped speaking in mid-sentence and asked, "Where is the man who is our example? He is not up front, he needs to be up front!" In order to let him know I was there, I raised my hand. He called me up front. He told one of the guys who was sitting in the front row to move and proceeded to tell me to sit there. I was both embarrassed and honored at the same time.

Even though that chaplain ruled with an iron fist, he

really honored those who loudly lived for Christ. However, within a year's time the administration also ran him out of there. I really sought God as to whether I should put in a transfer to where the chaplain was going. *I praise God that He led me to just be still.*

After that I had a few run-ins with Brother Pride. He had become even more prideful than he already was since the chaplain had appointed him the only elder of the services. What a preacher! He knew his bible. Pride was in a wheelchair and every morning he would go to one of the corners of the basketball courts and shout for the people to repent. Unfortunately, his life and temper didn't line up with everything that he preached, so there weren't too many people who even listened.

Brother Pride knew that God worked through me so whenever he was having problems with sickness or dealing with dreams, he would come to me. He shared a lot with me that he would not share with others.

Dealing with his temper was another side of our relationship and how he generally talked to people. Quite a few times Brother Pride and I got into arguments and would always call them the devil. One afternoon I went to talk to him about something that he had done and he got so mad at me that he actually stood up from his wheelchair as if he wanted to fight. The Spirit of God came upon me and I told him, "If you do not repent and turn from your wicked ways, God will remove you from the church!" When I said that I was thinking, and thus believed, that God would ride this brother out. (I left Level 4 a couple years later. Within a few months of being at the new facility, a man rode into the facility and told me that Brother Pride suffered a brain aneurism and had died. God opened my eyes and reminded me that I had prophesied that God was going to remove him from the church. I teared up and almost broke down. It had been the first time that God prophesied through me that He would, literally, remove someone if he did not repent. It actually happened within just a few months after I left him.)

About three months after the chaplain left, there were about 15 to 20 of us who got together and wanted to reestablish a leadership within the church. People were leaving the services because of the sin bashing method that Brother Pride had, and seeing he was the only coordinator, it happened every week. We invited anyone who wanted to come to the meeting, but there weren't too many people besides the 15 to 20 of us who even showed up. We came to the conclusion that we would have everyone there, and whoever wanted to participate, would write down 6 names of who they wanted to see up front leading the services.

Brother Tom was in charge of gathering the names. He told me that I was the most suggested. In many ways I was hoping that I wasn't named at all, for I was unsure if I was ready to lead. However, God showed me that I was ready by the voices of the people. All 6 of us came together and because the last true leader of the church, the chaplain, so named him, Brother Pride was left in a leadership position. After we all spoke up for the church concerning Brother Pride, he humbled himself and started to work with us instead of working against us.

It was during that time Karen was speaking of moving from Traverse City to right outside Las Vegas. We had never actually met face to face. We had then been writing for about 4 years. She told me that she was going to see me at least one time before she moved. At that time I was really seeking after the subjects of faith and the authority of the Word. I called her one night and she told me that she was able to sell all the small stuff, but that none of the big things were selling, and she was panicking.

I began to encourage Karen and we prayed. I loosed the angels and commanded the devil to take his hand off from her prosperity. I then told her to stop stressing, that all of her things were going to sell. She answered excitedly when I called her a week later, "Everything, and I mean everything sold the very next day after you prayed!" *Praise God!* I rejoiced with her both for getting the extra money and for not having to just throw stuff away. But, within my soul I was super nervous, for I still wanted a wife, and I clung to the possibility that she may still be the one.

The day arrived when she came in to see me for the first time. *So nervous!* My hands would not stop sweating. It was a nice visit, but my one goal was to find out if she was willing, or not, to make a commitment. We both wanted to kiss, but I knew within my spirit that I couldn't if she wasn't the one. I threw out a couple of hints during our visit, and then toward the end, I just asked her.

She said, "Why do you want to put us in a box?" I knew

right then and there that she was not the one and that I could not kiss her at the end of the visit. We finished talking and praying, then we got up and went to the door so the officer could let her out. At the beginning and the end of a visit, it was permissible to kiss our visitors (if that was our relationship with them), but nothing during the visit. I gave her a big hug and she put her face up toward mine (she stood only 5'2" tall); I embraced her even harder, but I would not kiss her. *I think that was one of the hardest things I had to face.* First, seeing how I have not kissed a woman in 14 years or so; and secondly, I so desperately wanted her to be my wife. *I thank God, that something that small, yet so powerful, I was able to get the victory over, for my first kiss belongs to the wife who God has for me. I know that's completely cheesy, but it's what I believe is pleasing to Him.*

Around that same time, I overheard someone telling a guy that the Dark Place was closing down. At first I didn't believe it, for I thought to myself, "What, another prison closed after, before leaving, I kicked the dust off my feet!" Sure enough, I saw the paperwork on it, the Dark Place was closing down. They moved all the prisoners there to an already closed prison, which they reopened, renaming it, The Dark Place. But the facility where I had been was closed. Wow!

Within a few months after that, a very blessed brother transferred back in from being at a Legal Writers course. He was talking about how great the place was from which he had just arrived. "Tables of brothers having bible studies every day in the units." He really boasted this place up.

About a week or so after he rode in, that brother moved into the cell right next to mine. After he had been there for about a month, I asked him what the facility looked like. He said, "Just like this one; more trees, but they are the same layout." *My spirit leaped with excitement.* Back in 2004, God had given me a vision about transferring into a new facility which looked just like Level 4, and He took it over with such a powerful anointing.

The Holy Spirit spoke, "That is the vision I gave you." I then asked, "Where were you? He answered, "Close to family". In excitement, I almost grabbed and shook him. That night I started to pray about the place, when The Boss came flooding into my mind. "Yes!" *I shouted excitedly at the Holy Spirit.*

When I went into work the next day, I asked The Boss if I could have a moment with him. He nodded and I closed the door behind me. I started out with, "I know that you are retiring sooner than later (thinking it would be 6 months to a year down the road), but I was wondering if you might be willing to try to get my name on the list to transfer closer to home?" He told me he would see what he could do. About two weeks later, he called me into his office and said, "You are on the list to go closer to home." "Yes! Thank you!" Once again, in appreciation, I almost threw my arms around him. *God bless that man.*

I was working one day and The Boss called me into the office and told me that I had to go back to the unit. When I got there I found that my cell mate was riding out to Level 1.

I thought it rather strange that I would be called back to the unit because my cell mate was riding out, *never happened before*. I headed back to work and as soon as I saw Isaac, my spirit came to life. I pulled him into a room and told him that my Bunkie was leaving and asked if he wanted to get moved in. I knew it was a long shot, but I believed that God was going to, once again, move within Isaac's life.

Isaac had the biggest smile on his face when I asked him to move in. He said, "I just told The Boss that I had to get out of the cell I was in and asked if he could send me to Level 1." Both of us hurried into The Boss's office and asked if he could pull some strings to get Isaac into my cell. A week later he was moving in. *Hallelujah to Jesus!*

For the first few weeks of having Isaac in the cell with me, I would continually encourage him, but I kept my distance for I did not want to seem like another man who was cramming doctrine down his throat. As he was able to get alone with God, and having a person to talk to about his faith (without being told he was wrong), he once again started to have a spark within his eyes. Soon, we were praying with each other, and began listening and feasting on every word of the teaching tapes by Kenneth Hagin and Kenneth Copeland. It was wonderful to see Isaac coming back into the place where I had first left him.

In the midst of all that, The Boss hired one more tutor, Brother Tom, a very blessed man of God. Since Isaac was the clerk and not a tutor, Tom was working with me. The Boss put Tom in charge of the refrigerators.

The way in which we had the class running was: two days of the week we would be cooking, the other three were classroom days. The first day of cooking would be a prep day. The students would get all of their groceries from the refrigerators, then come to me where they picked up everything they needed from the pantry. Both the refrigerators and the pantry would then be closed. Isaac was the one who corrected, and filled out all the paperwork. I loved working with those two men. To me it was a dream team, everything working like a well-oiled machine.

Then one day, as we all came into work, The Boss called us to his office and told us that he was retiring in three weeks. My heart sunk!

As I was trying to cope with the fact that My Boss was leaving, the old abandonment issue came flooding back into my soul. I found myself not knowing how to handle yet another person leave with whom I had grown so close.

Although I did not recognize it at the time, I found myself being tempted with stealing garbage bags for the trash can in my room. The officers back in the unit would not give us trash bags, and for the first time since I accepted Jesus into my heart I was stealing, and not just stealing but taking from someone that was very close to me. It was like I was blind to the reason. *I mean trash bags... really?*

Over and over again I found myself regretting not confessing that to The Boss before he retired. So many times, I have sought out, "Why?" *Why did I steal trash bags when all I had to do was ask him? I know he would have given them to me. Why did I not talk to him about it and get right with him?* After a year and a half, the Lord finally showed me why.

It was easier for me when I was on the streets before accepting Christ into my heart to push men away from my life; especially when I thought that they were about to leave me for whatever reason. A lot of the times I would do something like steal from them before they left in order to push them away so that I would be able to cope with them leaving. If I didn't do that, then in my mind it was my fault, no matter how good I tried to be. I always thought that I wasn't good enough and somehow I screwed up, being the cause of why they were leaving.

I found that coping mechanism was playing out again before The Boss retired. *For the first time, I am openly confessing and confronting this lie of abandonment which has kept me in guilt and condemnation. I know that Christ certainly has a better way to deal with issues from my past, than how I used to cope.* So, with The Boss retiring, being the first time where I knew that someone very close to me was leaving and having the time to process it, I fell right back into an old pattern of surviving. *Christ wants me to live, not survive like I had to do when I did not have Christ within my heart.*

The next three weeks were very sorrowful yet wonderful all at the same time. Each day, us tutors, would cook and eat something great, for *the food that the prison feeds us was usually pretty bad.* Toward the end we even cooked ribeye steaks on the grill. *Bitter sweet!*

The last day that The Boss was there, we were all eating and the school officer came through, stopped right next to me and asked if I wanted to be a barber. Without thinking, I said, "Heck, yes I do!" The guys laughed at me for that one. *What favor!* There I was, thinking that I wasn't going to have a decent job, and there came God just laying another dream job right into my lap. *What an awesome God!*

One afternoon I was told that I had a visitor. A brother from the church had come to see me. During that visit he told me that he would have to have surgery on his knee. Toward the end of our visit, right before we prayed, I told him that God could heal him. I went over some faith-strengthening scriptures, then I laid my hand upon the bad knee releasing the authority of the Word and commanding the pain to come out!

That brother stood up saying, "The pain is gone!" However, by the time that it took to get to the officer's desk, which was about 50 feet away, at least 5 times he said, "I can't believe it." God healed him for the pain was gone. At a later date he came back to see me, and told me that five days after he left me, the pain had returned and he had to have the surgery. *What a testimony of how powerful and true the Word of God is!* "A man's belly (or body) shall be satisfied with the fruit of his mouth; and with the increase of his lips shall he be filled. Death and life are in the power of the tongue; and they that love it shall eat the fruit thereof." (Proverbs 18:20-21) Then the book of Mark tells us, "If any man shall believe that those things which he says shall come to pass; he shall have whatsoever he says." (Mark 11:23) That brother had been healed, but a man shall have whatsoever he says, which in his case was, "I can't believe it", and five days later the pain came back. Faith! *We must walk, speak, think, sleep and live by faith!*

The passion of my heart was continuously being shown. I have found that I don't have a passion for the lost, even though when God brings someone into my life I will always preach the gospel to them, but my passion has always been for the church. Since being at my first transfer, I could not understand why people focused on bringing people to the faith and then introducing them into a tainted, sin stained, doubt-ridden church. No, my passion is to build and encourage the church itself that it "might be presented to Him as a glorious church, not having spot, or wrinkle or any such thing, but that it should be holy and without blemish." (Ephesians 5:27)

I am truly beginning to see why people have called me a prophet all of these years, and why God has given me so many revelations of foundational teachings, making Psalm 11:3 such a passion for my life and ministry. "If the foundations be broken up, what can the righteous do?" (Psalm 11:3) So many of the foundational teachings that Jesus, Peter, Paul and John preached are just not seen or taught today. What the Lord has been showing me, concerning calling me into the office of a prophet, was being more and more accepted and seen within my heart.

The definition, that I had found, of what a New Testament prophet is, has really opened my eyes to see that it is exactly what I am. "A prophet is one who speaks under divine inspiration, by the means of powerful exhortation to awaken the feelings and senses of the hearers." *Wow!* That has always fit everything that I have done and spoken.

While diligently searching through the book of Acts to see what a prophet is, I found that prophets were sent continuously; prophet after prophet is mentioned but evangelists, there was only one mentioned, and that was Philip... *The book of Acts gives us a really great visual of what prophets are today,* "And Judas and Silas, being prophets also themselves, exhorted the brethren with many words, and strengthened them." (Acts 15:32)

I found that the main function of the Old Testament prophet isn't even needed any more, seeing how they were the voice of God to the people. When people sought direction from God they would always go to the prophet, and the prophet would tell them what God's will and direction was for their lives. (1 Samuel 9:6-8) Now, under the New Covenant, we have the Holy Spirit, whose job is to direct and lead every born again believer, for, "My sheep hear my voice, and I know them, and they follow me: and I give unto them eternal life." (John 10:27-28) And, "Howbeit, when He, the Spirit of truth is come, He will guide you into all truth: for He shall not speak of Himself; but whatsoever He shall hear, that shall He speak: and shall tell you things to come." (John 16:13)

The purpose of the Old Testament prophet is gone. The purpose of the New Covenant prophet is to encourage and strengthen the church by divine inspiration and powerful revelations, having the mysteries of God revealed unto the sons of men, as it is now revealed unto His holy apostles and prophets by the Spirit." (Ephesians 3:3&5) My job is not to give direction within the people's lives; my job is to proclaim (preach) and teach the people how to live in the authority of the name of Jesus as true born again believers. *This was such a revelation to me.* It broke me free from always rejecting what God was calling me into because of some word that derived from bad teaching.

Back in Level 4 when I heard the word, 'Evangelist', I thought that a missionary was an evangelist, but that is not at all scriptural. A missionary (which is an apostle) is one who is sent. Not like the original apostles, but as one who lays foundational truth of the gospel of Christ, where Christ (The Anointed One and His anointing) is not accepted or known. It truly was an amazing moment for me when God brought all of that together within an hour's time. *God is awesome!*

Two days after The Boss retired, Isaac was transferred out to Level 1. I was so blessed that God had given me the desires of my heart in bringing Isaac back into the place where he, once again, was on fire for the Lord. God was moving so powerfully in my life and ministry.

As an example, I came into the church service one Sunday, and Brother Pride, who was coordinating the service that morning, approached me. He told me that a man had just asked him if we would pray for his wife. The woman had been in a coma for a couple of weeks and the doctors didn't hold out much hope. Brother Pride then asked me to open us up in prayer and to pray for that woman.

When it came time to pray I began as usual, and as I was praying for the woman, binding the enemy that was upon her, everyone started to shout! It was pretty awesome, even though that was usually how the people responded to my prayers, yet, I knew something was different.

The next day, an older black man came up to me, grabbed my arm and started to shake my hand. I wasn't sure who the guy was, but hey, it was okay! Then the man told me that he was the one who asked Brother Pride to pray for his wife, and that he heard that I was the one who actually prayed for her. He told me something that blessed me.

The man said, "Yesterday morning at about 10:20, I was told that my wife awoke from her coma, and as she was pulling out cords from her arms, she sat straight up yelling, 'You can't take me!' (We had prayed at about 10:10!) I asked him if he was a Christian. He told me, "No, I am a Jehovah Witness." It really made sense why she would come out of the coma yelling, the devil had her at the gates of hell. I don't know if that man, or his wife, ever gave their lives to Jesus as the Christ, but I know that God answers prayer in mighty and powerful ways.

One day as I came back to the cell from working at the barber shop, I saw that I had a new cell mate. He was a younger black man, who went by the name of 'Joey'. I found out by another man, who Brother Joey had moved away from, that he was a gang leader. Within two weeks' time, God so wonderfully moved within that young man's life. He accepted Jesus Christ into his heart and brought another one of his friends to me. He, too, accepted Jesus Christ. It was amazing to see God moving within the two young men's lives.

I would often walk the yard with both of those men and disciple them in the ways of the kingdom of God. One afternoon as I was walking with another, both of them came up to me with big smiles on their faces. Almost in unison, they both said, "We have something to tell you." Each of them had renounced the gang life! Praise God!

Brother Joey was called to the desk by the officers one day and told he had to switch cells with another inmate. An hour or so later, an older white man, who was having problems with his cell mate came walking in. Brother Joey slowly started to fall back into the same old life style. It broke my heart to see, but I knew that God had him and no matter how hard he may fall, at the right time, God was going to bring him back.

My new cell mate was Joey's biological brother. He said that he and Joey were raised up in a Catholic family, and believed in Jesus Christ as Lord and Savior. Within a month, my cell mate received a job as a Classification Clerk. Classification was in charge of all jobs on the compound, as well as, keeping updates on all the ride in's and ride out's. I told him that I wouldn't be there long seeing how I was being transferred closer to home. He informed me, "No, that probably won't happen, for the only ride out's going there are from the segregation." I fully believed that God was going to fulfill His vision and Word to me about moving closer to home. Everything in the natural seemed like it was not going to happen, but faith calls those things that are not as if they were, so I continually told people that I was transferring.

While in the process of waiting for God's promise to be fulfilled, I was asked by the school officers if I would be willing to help put on a demonstration for a new menu which was being introduced by a private vendor who was hired to feed the prison population. *What an honor!* The officer told me that the reason the vendor was using our facility was because there were no Food Tech classes being held there.

For three days I worked with the company's head chef, who they flew up from Florida to cook and present the new dishes which were already being used in other states. Some of the dishes were not bad; others left a lot to be desired. Either way I knew that even if accepted and brought into use, *none of the dishes would be the same being prepared here!* Since Tom and I were The Boss's tutors we both were asked to help, it was an awesome experience. Working in the kitchen during the day until 4 in the afternoon, and being the barber at night, made for some really long days. *Yet, once again, favor!*

Because I was not transferring like I was calling forth, people began mocking my faith. *It is amazing how people who are called to walk by faith, mocks the ones who operate in faith.*

Then one day I ran into an officer who I knew from my first five years there. I pulled him to the side and asked if he would be willing to speak to the Transfer Coordinator for me. Officers were not supposed to show favoritism in any way toward a prisoner, but I just had God tugging at my heart to speak to this officer. He and I always got along well, for God would always grant me favor, and operate through me in mighty ways. The officer said he would see what he could do.

Within a couple of weeks' time, on a Monday morning I was coming into the unit and my counselor called me over to say that I was riding out that week. He even told me where I was going and gave me the three digit code for the facility which was closer to home! I was in awe, especially since, because of security purposes, prisoners are never supposed to know when or where they are going. But *here was this man (who doesn't even like to talk to prisoners) telling me when and where I was going!*

When I got back to my cell, I told my bunk mate that I would be gone that week, but doubt poured out of him. I believe it was for two reasons. First, he would continually tell me that I was the best Bunkie that he had in all of his twenty one years of doing time. Secondly, naturally speaking, he just was not seeing it anywhere on paper.

I had my answer. *I always go back to the promise of God which says, "The trial of your faith, being much more precious than of gold that perishes, though it be tried with fire, might be found unto praise and honor and glory at the appearing of Jesus Christ...receiving the end of your faith..."* (1 Peter 1:7, and 9) I was receiving the end of what I was believing in, my transfer closer to home. *Praise God!*

Two days later I was called to the desk and told to pack up my property. I already had everything packed. From the moment I spoke to that counselor I acted in faith. The next morning I was told to go to the control center and wait for the bus.

9

CLOSE TO FAMILY

I was completely excited, but found myself questioning if I was, in fact, going closer to home. The bus pulled into another correctional facility and my heart dropped. I began telling myself, "This is not where I am going." Then I heard the guards telling us that we were at a drop off point, and that we would be shuttled out from there to where we were going. *Thank God!*

We exited the bus and walked toward a huge warehouse. The guard standing in front of it saw me and shouted the name of my hometown and the facility where I was headed. My spirit leaped and I found myself saying under my breath, "I knew it!"

Throughout my stint in prison, there had been so many people who had said that the place where they were told they were going, was not at all the place they went. I had to bind that doubt, for *God is always faithful.*

About an hour later, along with about 15 others, they called me, and I boarded the bus. Another 2 hours later, we finally pulled up to the close to home correctional facility. *I am so excited, yet nervous.* It is always nerve wracking going into a new facility, not knowing who your bunk mate is, and many other things.

Finally, after waiting two more hours in a small room each of us, one at a time, saw the nurse. My time came up and I answered whatever questions she asked, then was sent to my unit. I exited the doorway and entered the compound, saw trees everywhere! *So nice!* Most facilities don't have any trees. I entered into my unit, received my key and went toward my new cell.

As I was walking up to my cell, a light skinned black gentleman, in his mid-50's, came whipping out of the cell and asked if I was going to 59-top and wanted to know how long I had been doing time. I told him, "Yes" and "17 years". He then said, "Okay then, you know what's what"; then he left.

I entered the cell and saw Muslim stuff all over the place. Most Muslims are not really serious about their faith; I began to wonder where this man was in his belief. I found out about an hour later when the man came back. He told me that he was about to pray, and then began to tell me what I can and cannot do while he is praying. Right then and there, I knew it was not going to be a nice smooth stay.

After count cleared, I immediately went down to the day rooms looking for all of the believers that my dear brother back in Level 4 had told me about. At one table there were two men with open bibles. I went to the table and asked if they were Christians. They said, "Yes, we are." *Hallelujah!* I found out that one of them was just a few cells down from mine.

I was called to the desk the following day to retrieve

my property. All that morning I was putting everything away and settling in. That afternoon, I went out to the big yard and immediately started praying and claiming revival in my new place.

The first week of being there, I was able to get my kite to the chaplain in time to be placed on the call-out for the Christian services. I was told that the services are at nighttime. *How cool!* Every other place I've been, it's always been in the morning. In this place was a brand new chapel which was built right on the compound. In every other facility, the services were either in a school room, or in the gym.

I entered the chapel for the first time and, *wow!* The seats were super nice, having really thick and wide cushions. Before the service actually started, in came about 20 volunteers. I watched every one of them take a seat right in the midst of the prisoners. That would never happen at any other facility I've been to, the volunteers are to sit up front facing the prisoners. They could not intermingle at all, except for at the beginning and the end of the service. *Not here though!*

By the time everyone came in and the service began, there were about 150 prisoners packed in. *What a sight! I am used to anywhere from 30 to 60 people.* At the Dark Place once we got to 104. *Here Christians are everywhere!* The minister got up and gave an anointed message. *Come to find out, actual pastors come in here. Amazing!* And then, the secondary services. *Wow!* So many of them, *there is some type of Christian service going on every day.*

During one of the Sunday night services, as it was getting over with, I saw someone walking out, which brought dread within my soul. It was the chaplain's clerk who had created so much havoc at the Dark Place. I immediately started to pray and bind whatever fear was trying to get in. My mom came up to visit and I told her about it and asked her to also pray. *I know that there is nothing impossible for God!*

So, I was praying that God would somehow restore the friendship that the brother and I once had; that when we meet face to face again that there be no anger or resentment at all within either of us.

A week or two later, I entered one of the bible study rooms in the school building, and I saw him sitting with his back toward me. The first thing that came to mind was to turn around and leave. I told myself that would not be faith. I encouraged myself in what I had been praying for and went over to him. As soon as he looked up and recognized me, a big smile came upon his face. He stood up and we greeted one another with a huge hug. Just as I had wanted, nothing was said of the Dark Place. God had answered every one of my prayers in reconciling me with that brother. *We don't talk a whole lot, but praise God there is no strife at all between us. I so love my God!*

Within the next few weeks I met many brothers who, almost all, were in different units. About three months before I arrived, the facility made the entire C-unit a sex offenders unit, as well as, putting all the urban ministry students who did not have a sex case over in A-unit. The program is a four year seminary class. The B-unit which I was in, didn't have many believers, at least, not dedicated believers.

I was told by a couple of people that due to the facility making C-unit a sex offenders unit, it created an atmosphere of violence. The truth (which many lie about) of their crimes came out, and because of it, many of the gangs had started to stab a lot of people. They would use an area that had a lot of trees as cover from the cameras, and would then wait until the shift change. They would then lure their victim out there and violate them. Of course, that strengthened the attitudes of the gangs to begin strong arming people who were new or looked like a target (young and innocent looking). *As far as I was concerned, all of that was about to change.*

One thing I found within the compound to be very overwhelming was a spirit of sorrow. The Warden, who was a sold out Christian, had been forced into early retirement because he had taken a vacation with a prisoner's family. The prisoner of that family, started waving pictures around of his family and the Warden, together in Las Vegas. One of the Deputy Wardens, who did not like her boldness in Christ or the favor that she gave to prisoners, contacted the state, and after 45 years of service, she was told to retire. Everyone who knew her was still very hurt over such a huge loss. She was the life of the facility. *I thank God, though, because I've found that Jesus alone is Life! This is His Church and it does not belong to the Warden. God heals His people and I was believing for revival. I set my heart toward the healing of the people here and I'm praying for His mighty work.*

After lunch, every day I would walk the track on the big yard, praying for healing and revival, binding every plot and plan that Satan had, and asking that it would stop, in the name of Jesus!

Within the first month of going to the bible study in the unit I found that the brother who was being taught was super hungry for the foundational truths of God's Word. However, the brother leading the study was caught up in his own abilities. It amazed me that regardless of how much the brother leading the study wanted to, and tried to receive the spiritual dynamics in his life, he just could not get past his soulish nature. While the brother who just wanted to learn, grew by leaps and bounds. To see the huge contrast between those two men was an eye opener. I have found that, as a whole, this is the contrast within the church.

One day during the unit bible study, a brother who was in my unit, came up in conversation in a negative way. All I heard about that brother was a whole lot of bad things. Although, every time I saw or heard him speak at a bible study, he was on fire for God. I just was not connecting what I was hearing to what I was seeing. Rather than just taking everyone's word about him, I took the time to get to know that brother. What a ministry and heart the man had for Jesus! I invited him to the bible study, but he told me "No". Then he said, "While in A-unit they kicked me out of the unit's bible study." I still did not see what everyone was talking about. All I knew was that God had given me a passion to disciple that brother.

He started coming to the unit bible study with us and the study grew from 6 to 15 within just a few weeks. That brother drew people in. Then one day, his temper showed up and he lost it. He went off on another man. He just lost sight of who he was in Christ and the devil came out in full swing! I then got a glimpse of what everyone had been talking about. His anger started to come out more often. I refused to give up on that brother. I knew that God had called him and had given him such an anointing to draw people to Christ. But, within time, strife started to enter into the unit bible study because of him being very opinionated and passionate. I found that his anger would spoil whatever he wanted to do for Jesus. About two to three weeks later he transferred out. *I still believe that once he surrenders all of his anger and bitterness to Jesus, that God is going to do great things through that brother.*

At the time, God was moving powerfully through me and people were being healed of pain and sickness. One brother who was young in faith, came to the table, sick as could be. I told him what the Word said and then asked if I could lay hands on him and pray; he accepted the offer. I laid hands on him and bound the sickness in Jesus' name, and commanded the authority of the Word to heal his body. The next day he told me that he had been completely healed, saying, "Many people have laid their hands on me, and nothing ever happened; but yesterday, I was healed!"

Another brother at the unit bible study came walking in with a limp. I asked him what happened. He told me, "I sprained my ankle while playing soccer." I told him what the

Word said and offered to pray over him and he accepted. I laid my hand on his swollen ankle and commanded the pain and swelling to come out in Jesus name. That brother stood up and his pain was gone. Immediately, he began to jump up and down, saying, "The pain is gone! Hallelujah to Jesus!"

After chow one night, a couple of us were sitting at a table in the day room and a guy came up to us who wasn't even a believer. He told us his bunk mate needed to get with people who would steer him in the right direction in life. A day or two later, after dinner, we were again in the day room and met the man's bunk mate. After about 45 minutes of ministering to him, God so wonderfully took over our conversation and the brother accepted Jesus Christ as His Lord and Savior.

Throughout the weeks that followed, we found that the new brother had a real problem. He lied to everyone. We called him "Charlie". He had been in gangs his entire life, but had since separated from the organization he had been part of, but he was having problems with the gang at the existing facility. It was discovered that the young man, when at another facility, went to that gang's leader and told him that he would pay 50 dollars a month for protection, and the gang at the present facility was demanding collection. When Charlie asked the brother what the truth was, he lied to him, but when they went together to the leader of the facility's gang, the truth came out and Charlie was almost put under the bus. *Praise God for His intervention.*

A few days later we were sitting at the table and the

Spirit again showed me a lying spirit in the young brother. Failing to recognize it was God, I ignored it and didn't take the opportunity right then and there to command it out of him. The anointing to see that spirit left. I repented to God for missing it and asked that He would give me another opportunity to cast that devil out of the young brother.

God gave me the opportunity the next day. We were sitting at a table by ourselves, and, once again, the Spirit came upon me. I told the young man that he had a spirit of lying upon him and that it needed to come out. He said he had always wanted deliverance from that. I commanded the lying spirit to come out of him and as I did so, in Jesus' name, the guy's face changed right in front of me. A peace came flooding into his eyes. It was amazing! That night he was called to the officer's desk and was told to pack up his property. The next day he transferred out. *God is awesome!*

During that time, the Spirit was moving mightily, there were people healed, brothers received the baptism of the Holy Spirit and began to speak in other tongues, and deliverances were being granted. It was an amazing time!

On the flip side of the amazing things God was doing, it was a completely different story within my cell. First, I had a bottom bunk, which meant I could never sit up straight without hitting the top bunk with my head. *So, as you can imagine, I do not like bottom bunks.* Then, every morning at 6, whether I was awake or not, my bunk mate would get up and loudly pray. For the first month or so, I didn't mind it, but every day, 5 times a day, out loud, he would pray. He was a very loud TV watcher; he would talk to his television as if it heard him. If he was passionate about what he was watching, he would continually talk to the set. When there was no response, and in order to get his point across, all the louder he would talk.

I dreaded seeing my bunk mate turn on his music for I knew it would be only a matter of time before he started to loudly sing. It got to the point where it was so bad, I told him, "Dude, your singing is horrible!" His response actually made me laugh. He said, "If I sang well, then I wouldn't be in here!" I couldn't argue with that logic.

That man had another side; he had such a giving heart. He wasn't a bad guy at all, just those few things covered up all of his good traits. I tried to have a discussion with him one day about our faiths. It ended up with him standing on his feet as if he was standing before God (yelling, so I would know how serious he was), "I will tell God that I served Him and Him alone and that I know He doesn't have a Son or any equals!" I just let go of the conversation.

In time, I found myself allowing that man's spirit to get me down. I tried multiple times to move out of the cell and into another, but the administration would not move me. I was constantly having people ask who my bunk mate was, and when I told them, each and every one of them would say the same thing, "Oh, man, I feel sorry for you."

Everything that man did was loud whether in or outside the cell. I remember one time after he was done playing chess with someone, he didn't like how the guy played or something, and followed him everywhere he went yelling and shouting at him. If the other guy went into a different day room, my bunk mate followed and continued to yell. Everyone knew of him, and nobody wanted to lock with him.

One night while I was in prayer, the Lord told me that I was not going to leave until I preached the gospel to that man. Knowing that my bunk mate grew up in a Christian household, I figured that he already knew it. Although, when I thought back on my own life, I never grew up in church, and I never once heard that Jesus Christ died for my sins, until I read the bible in the county jail. I prayed that God would give me an opportunity to preach the gospel to him.

The day came, the opportunity was presented, and I took it. Every time I started to preach about the gospel, he would cut me off and turn the direction of the topic. Finally, I said something that I was not at all expecting to say. I told him, "The Koran is a counterfeit. It was written after the bible and every story in the Koran is twisted from the truth of what is actually in the Bible." He didn't even get mad; however, with many words, he did try to convince me to believe on the Koran. Then I touched upon the love of God and he flipped out, "Don't tell me about the love of God! I don't want to hear about that!" On and on he went. I ended the conversation after that one. I laughed because he didn't even get mad when I called the Koran a counterfeit; but he flipped out when I told him about the love of God!

During that time, I was offered a job pushing a laundry cart. I had taken the job because it paid more money than the job I had as a porter, and I loved it. On Monday, Wednesday and Friday, I worked 5 minutes in the morning, then 5 minutes in the afternoon, and was paid for five days. I was able to use my time in the yard to edify and encourage others. That job was short lived.

The unit officer, the same one who gave me the laundry cart job, offered me a Handicap Pushing job. When I asked who it was he told me it was Mr. Johns. I knew of him and there was nothing within me that was telling me, 'no', so I said, 'yes'. *Again, God's favor.* At about $40 - $50 a month, it was one of the highest paid jobs on the compound. Once I got the detail to start working, I went to introduce myself to him.

I stood in his doorway and told him my name. Immediately he pointed to his bulletin board and said, "You know Him, too, don't you?" I looked to where he was pointing and saw that hanging there was a picture of Jesus. I responded with, "Yes, I do my dear brother!"

A month or two after that, Mr. Johns told me that his bunk mate was about to go home. We talked to his counselor about me being able to move in with Mr. Johns. The counselor said, "Anthony, if I am here and if they don't put someone else in there before I can put your name in the computer, then 'yes'. *Hallelujah to Jesus. I may just be getting out of this cell that I'm in!* Mr. Johns' bunk mate left, we talked to his counselor and everything seemed like it was a go. That morning I told my bunk mate that I would be moving and told him to see if he could find someone he wanted to take my place. God worked awesomely! I was able to move and my bunk mate was able to get the person he wanted. Not only that, but He gave me a top bunk, too! *Yes!*

What a difference from the last cell. It was so peaceful. Every day at 2:15 p.m. when the yard opened, I would bring Mr. Johns out to walk. Since his stroke the only way for him to get out of the wheelchair was for him to walk while pushing it. At first, I had to sit in it as he pushed, because when he would lean down on the handles the whole chair would tip up on him. Then after a few months I had him push it without me in it. Every stage was a mental block more than anything else for him. Praise God that after 8 months, he received a very nice walker with a seat on it and they took away his wheelchair. *Hallelujah to Jesus!* It was interesting how so many people would speak against me having him walk, as though I was doing him wrong or something. It was as if people in general, wanted to see him in that wheelchair for the rest of his life. But, as we pushed forward, and as Mr. Johns would get a little bit quicker, the mindset of people began to change. They started praising him, rather than ridiculing me. *I thank God, for now, though slowly, he is walking with the aid of his walker, and people are praising him. I love to see how God turns people's hearts.*

One day, as we were coming back to the unit and Mr. Johnn was pushing me, Levi stopped us saying, "Brother, I have been looking for you all day. I need prayer for my foot. It's been hurting like crazy." I reached down from the wheelchair and laid my hand on his foot, and commanded the pain to come out in the name of Jesus. Then I removed my hand. Levi said, "Thank you" and left. The next day as Mr.

Johns and I were walking, Levi was walking down the side walk to go to work and saw us. He began jumping up and down on his foot, claiming, "I am completely healed!" *God is amazing!*

I would like to share another testimony concerning that same brother. I was walking and when I saw Levi, and a couple of other brothers at a table, I headed over there to greet them. Levi gave me a hug and even before I was seated, proceeded to tell me of a situation that he was in. Once seated, he continued by saying, "I have a strange prayer request for you. I know God answers your prayers. It's strange, because I am not asking for healing, but rather for my heart to go into whatever it is doing and stay so the doctor can hear it."

He continued, "Every time my heart acts up and I head over to the health care, it stops before the doctor can listen. So, I am asking that you pray for it to start and not stop until it is checked out." I said, "Okay." *For I believe that God meets us at where our faith is. So, if this is where Levi's faith is, then who am I to say anything different?* I laid my hands on him and prayed that whenever Levi's heart began to act up that it wouldn't quit until the doctor was able to listen to it. I finished in Jesus name and believed it was done. Within a weeks' time, Brother Levi came running up and began to tell me how his heart started to act up. He had gone to the health care, and it continued. They took him to the hospital and it was still going. The doctors at the hospital were able to run tests on it. He finished by saying that his heart continued to do what it was doing for four and a half hours. That brother was so excited. *God is amazing!*

During that period of getting back to where I wanted to be with God, I went into the day room and I saw a man whom I had never seen before. He had a bible in front of him and the pages were covered with all sorts of notes he had written down in different colors. I was immediately drawn to him. I found out he was going home in a couple of weeks. I spent as much time with him as I could. He would share what God had shown him through his readings.

That brother told me that he had read every single book, whether commentary or teaching, hundreds of books, from the chaplain's library in the facility where he came from. Being locked up and in the same place for three years, he had a beautiful gift of being able to see so many examples using the Old Testament scriptures. It was really amazing.

During our conversations, which were usually morning, noon and night I, too, would share with him what God had revealed to me through my studying of the Word. (For there were no bible studies happening in the unit during that time.) There was one brother who was drawn to join us as often as he could. He was an older man who introduced himself as Brother Eli (Eli was actually his last name). He was so hungry to see revival, which of course, once again, got me excited.

The time came for Brother David to go home. What sweet fellowship we had together. About a week later, Eli came to me and asked if I would be willing to teach him everything that I had been shown by the Spirit of God. Eli said, "I only want to listen. God is telling me that you are the one who I am to learn from."

There was another young brother who I had ministered to once or twice on the track who was with Eli, and he, too, asked me to disciple him. That young brother was just as hungry for the Word as Eli. The three of us started to get together every morning, from 8:15 to 9:00, Monday through Saturday. The Spirit led me to speak on nothing other than the foundational teachings which He had revealed to me. As we were coming together, God was moving so powerfully, revealing things to me as I was speaking, which had never happened to me before. We went over faith, righteousness, His cross, our crosses, His authority in us, the true gospel of Christ, and the fruit of the Spirit...revelation after revelation was being poured out. In the midst of all that the Spirit led me to start a bible study back up during the evenings before chow, on Tuesdays and Thursdays. It grew from 4 to 15. *Now there are about 12 of us who show up every time we meet, just feasting on what God has for His people.*

For the first time in my walk, I find that I am not running from the studies like I have every other place I've been. I used to deny everyone who called me a teacher. "No, I am a preacher! Not a teacher." I would get frustrated and begin to draw away from the studies, and shortly afterward everyone else would also break apart. *Here, I am not finding that at all. Actually, I am finding that God has anointed me with a gift of teaching. It is amazing!*

This is just the beginning of what God is doing within me, and through me, meeting the needs of His people. To His glory, and His glory alone.

EPILOGUE

Throughout the eighteen years that I have been going through the "prison chapter" of my life, I have found that God uses many things to reach the hearts of men who are locked behind bars and fences. In here, almost all, especially the lost, have very hardened hearts toward people and religion. So, if people don't see Christ first, they won't listen to what anyone has to say about God.

Like in the free world, there are many "gods", people either believe or don't, but as Christians we serve the only God who unconditionally loves us. As prisoners of Christ, we help to spread the gospel more effectively in here. There are a few ways that we must be helped in order to more effectively spread the gospel.

First, the people in here make anywhere from $6 to $40 per month. The majority average $15 to $20 monthly, which is eaten up by basic needs and toiletries. I have used this to my advantage in reaching the lost by giving people soap, coffee, or food. I will never forget one of the guys to whom I gave soap. When he took it his eyes began to water and he told me that nobody had ever before given him anything... NOBODY! In order to preach to him the real love of God, a bar of soap was my way into that man's heart. I say the real love of God because many people preach God's love, but there are numerous stipulations and conditions to receiving it. *God's love is unconditional.*

In here, gang members are restricted by the administration. Most cannot have a job or even use our email system to write letters. In order to survive, many times they are forced to steal. It always amazes me how God can open a huge door for effective witnessing via food or coffee.

Now, even though not one prisoner did anything good and upright to get sentenced to here, many are whole-heartedly serving Christ. Even with believers out in the free world, there are many who operate from a "prisoners deserve to be in prison" mentality. The church needs to break free from that fear and those judgmental thoughts. I have spoken with several volunteers (people who come into the prisons for our main services or for Christian classes) who have said we are nothing like what they first thought. Their perceptions were dissolved and friendships were created as they got to know us. I'd like to point out a couple of things.

First, our Old Testament examples were in prison for being a menace to society. Even though Paul and Peter were preaching the gospel, it went against those who enforced the rules and laws of their day. Paul himself pretty much created a riot every place he went.

Secondly, in the beginning, the "prison system" was created to rehabilitate and convert men from their evil ways by leading them to Christ, and teaching them how to live a changed life as a Christian. That was the intent in founding the prisons, until greed became involved, and the idea surfaced that prisons could make a lot of money. Law itself tells us that ALL crime is commercial. *My prayer is that the*

Church returns to the original idea and vision of what the prisons are for...a means of saving the lost and to teach men and women how to live loudly for Jesus.

I would like to share some ways where the Christians in the free world can help us who are incarcerated, to more effectively, spread the gospel. Statistics tell us there is a person from each family who is in, or has been, in prison. Therefore, chances are every person knows someone, (whether a cousin, uncle, brother, sister, daughter, son, father, or mother,) who is, or has been, in prison.

What is the Church out in the free world doing to help win the lost who are hidden behind these bars and fences? The author of Hebrews tells us, "Remember them that are in bonds (chains or prison), as (if) bound with them..." (Hebrews 13:3)

Jesus said to them on His right side, "...Come, you blessed of the Father, inherit the kingdom prepared for you from the foundation of the world: for I was hungry, and you gave me meat: I was thirsty, and you gave me drink: I was a stranger, and you took me in: Naked, and you clothed me: I was sick, and you visited me: I was in PRISON, and you came unto me." When the righteous (those on His right side) asked when they did these things unto Him, He replied, "Verily I say unto you, inasmuch as you have done it unto one of the least of these my brothers, you have done it unto Me." But when the unrighteous (those on His left side) asked Jesus the same question, He said, "Verily I say unto you, inasmuch as you did it not to one of the least of these, you did it not to Me." (Matthew 25: 31-45)

One way in which to help is by sending encouragement letters. As previously mentioned, there is probably someone you know who is imprisoned, and they may, or may not, be a Christian. By sharing your faith through a letter, you could be the one who shows up for a prisoner. That simple act would not only show the love of Jesus, but it could bring them to accept Christ into their hearts. I know a man who had just came back to prison and got into a fight with another prisoner. He ended up choking, almost to death, the other prisoner. While alone in solitary confinement, a letter was slid underneath the door. It was from a woman he didn't know. In the letter she told him that Jesus loves him and that He does care about and for him. That day, that man accepted Christ into his heart.

Paul tells us that one plants and one waters, but it is God who gives the increase. (1 Corinthians 3:6-8) You may just be the one who waters the seeds that have been planted. Where it takes root and accomplishes the intent of God's love toward them is being born-again, when they accept Christ into their heart.

You could also begin to visit the prisoner who you know, literally showing them the love of Jesus. You probably won't be able to just show up, there are necessary steps that would need to be followed. You might have to be approved, so ask the prisoner how to get on their visiting list.

Another way for the Christian community to help is by donating soft or hard covered new study bibles. However, for obvious reasons, there are strict rules which must be observed. **The rule is: Only new bibles are allowed to be sent to prisoners**, or to the chaplain. Bibles are to be ordered and shipped directly to the prisoner, along with a gift certificate, from Amazon.com or from the publisher, **not a bookstore. NO USED BIBLES** can be sent to the prisoners. Every state is a little different, having their own policies, but you can find out from the prisoner what procedures would need to be taken. (Shipped orders should include: prisoner's first and last name along with their inmate ID number.)

Financially is another way in which to help prisoners. Many have no one on the outside, but here again, strict compliance to the policies and procedures must be observed. One cannot just send someone in prison a check or currency, it has to be done in accordance with that prison's rules and guidelines.

In summary, believers in here beg for help every day. There are so many asking for prayer that they might be reconciled back to their families. Some brothers are pleading for a good study bible, but they are just not provided. Many prisons have no Christian classes where volunteers come in and God's people are crying out for help. To help meet that cry, will you be the hand that reaches out into some of the darkest places of the world?

I believe that mass revivals will break out first in the prisons fulfilling God's word. "For consider your calling, brothers: not many of you were wise according to worldly standards, not many were powerful, and not many were of noble birth. But God chose what is foolish in the world to shame the wise; God chose what is weak in the world to shame the strong; God chose what is low and despised in the world, even things that are not, to bring to nothing things that are, so that no human being might boast in the presence of God." (1 Corinthians 1:26-29) Jesus said that he did not come for the righteous, but to save that which was lost. (Matthew 18:11 & Luke 19:10) *And, we certainly have lost our way.*

My mom cried out when she heard that I was looking at natural life. "I did not raise my son this way!" I'm sure that many of the parents of those who are in here have cried out the same way over their sons and daughters. Will you be the one to break the heavy yoke that is being carried on the shoulders of a prisoner who lost his or her way?

We need you to be that hand for us. We need the Church to awaken to the fact that many in the body of Christ are in the darkest places of the world. Where we reside your help is needed to brightly shine God's light.

ACKNOWLEDGEMENTS

First, and most of all, I thank God for being my Lord, Savior, teacher, and guide. I'm thankful He did not answer my prayers by sending someone to disciple me; rather, kept me alone, where I could seek answers from Him, not man or traditional teachings. I thank Him for always being my Father, best friend, and the Great Revealer of His mysteries which formed and shaped me into the man of God that I am today.

Also, I want to thank my dear mother, my mom. There was a time when I didn't even want to acknowledge she was family. I didn't realize, that all my life she was there for me and, *now reconciled*, has become my closest friend.

Bill and Roger, thank you both. Each of you inspired me to write my story and were a huge support for my ministry.

ABOUT THE AUTHOR

Everything changed when ANTHONY KREHN came to know the Lord Jesus. The difference it made in his life was like going from night to day. Once he began experiencing the love God had for him he asked everyone to stop referring to him as 'Tony' and call him, 'Anthony', which was God's name for him.

Throughout the years, Author, Anthony Krehn, had prayed that God would send a disciple into his life. Although God did not answer his prayer the way this author thought best, God did mightily answer with the Holy Spirit.

Like the apostle Paul, Anthony claims that he was not taught by man. Rather, all things were revealed unto him by the Holy Spirit. His passion is to build the Church up and to see all of God's people become the reflection of who Jesus is to the world.

This author longs to experience and to know God in ways which far surpasses one's own thoughts of possibilities. As in 2 Corinthians 3:2, he desires to be found in God's Spirit where he becomes a living epistle, read and known of all men, and so hidden that when people hear or see him, they only see and hear Jesus. "Jesus in an Anthony suit", he says.

ANTHONY KREHN strives to live by the scripture: "Now thanks be unto God who always causes us to triumph in Christ, and makes manifest the fragrance of His knowledge by us in every place." (2 Corinthians 2:14-16) "If the Son therefore shall make you free, you shall be free indeed.(John 8:36) .That is why he titled his testimony, "Set Free".

Anthony Krehn, in authorizing his testimony shares his experience in coming to know God in ways which far surpasses ones own thoughts of possibilities.

SET FREE

By: Brother Anthony

When I would go to see him he never shared any of these stories; he just preached

Dont understand the prophecy thing on Chap 3

Was it Jim Danenburg who led A to Jesus?

CPSIA information can be obtained
at www.ICGtesting.com
Printed in the USA
FFHW010704090119
50124299-55004FF